Can't Play
Won't Play

of related interest

Self-Esteem Games for Children
Deborah Plummer
Illustrations by Jane Serrurier
ISBN 978 1 84310 424 7

Integrated Yoga
Yoga with a Sensory Integrative Approach
Nicole Cuomo
ISBN 978 1 84310 862 7

Understanding Motor Skills in Children with Dyspraxia, ADHD, Autism, and other Learning Disabilities
A Guide to Improving Coordination
Lisa A. Kurtz
ISBN 978 1 84310 865 8

Caged in Chaos
A Dyspraxic Guide to Breaking Free
Victoria Biggs
ISBN 978 1 84310 347 9

Can't Play
Won't Play

Simply Sizzling Ideas
to get the Ball Rolling
for Children with Dyspraxia

Sharon Drew and Elizabeth Atter

Illustrations by Elizabeth Atter

Jessica Kingsley Publishers
London and Philadelphia

First published in 2008
by Jessica Kingsley Publishers
116 Pentonville Road
London N1 9JB, UK
and
400 Market Street, Suite 400
Philadelphia, PA 19106, USA

www.jkp.com

Library of Congress Cataloging in Publication Data
Drew, Sharon.
 Can't play won't play : simply sizzling ideas to get the ball rolling for children with dyspraxia / Sharon
Drew and Elizabeth Atter.
  p. cm.
 ISBN-13: 978-1-84310-601-2 (pb : alk. paper) 1. Apraxia--Patients--Recreation. 2. Exercise for
children. 3. Play. I. Atter, Elizabeth (Elizabeth Anne), 1959- II. Title.
 RJ496.A63D74 2008
 618.92'8552--dc22
                                        2007030159

British Library Cataloguing in Publication Data
A CIP catalogue record for this book is available from the British Library

ISBN 978 1 84310 601 2

Printed and bound in the United States by
Thomson-Shore, Inc.

CONTENTS

ACKNOWLEDGEMENTS

We would like to thank all our colleagues in Health and Education who have shared their ideas and helped shape our knowledge.

A big thanks goes to all the children and their families who we have met along the way who willingly test drove our theories and advice.

We would like to thank our parents for their love, support and encouragement throughout our careers.

Last but not least we would like to thank James and Becks who have posed for photos and drawings and been our guinea pigs as they have been growing up. Of course we cannot forget Tim and Martin who have had to live on microwave dinners...thanks boys! XXX

1 INTRODUCTION... USUALLY A REALLY GOOD PLACE TO START!

As two very experienced therapists we have worked for many years with children who have difficulty with everyday play, games and activities due to poor co-ordination and motor control.

Sharon is an occupational therapist (OT) and Liz is a physiotherapist (PT). We are frequently asked to enable children to join in the same activities as their friends and classmates. This might be at school, at their local leisure centre or just in the street or park. Parents want to be able to help but might not know how to. Whilst it would be great if all of the children who experience difficulty with co-ordination could see an OT or PT, the sad reality is that this is not always possible.

Experience, and now research, is showing that if parents and carers are given the right information and ideas, they can often be their child's best 'therapist'. The aim of this book, therefore, is to provide a practical resource for parents and carers to dip in and out of to help children with some of the more common activities they report as wanting to improve.

The book is laid out using the following icons to help focus on particular aspects:

⚠ Warning triangle to indicate safety notes.

❓ Question mark to indicate frequently asked questions.

💡 Light bulb to indicate tips and hints for you to try.

R Letter R to indicate resources and information that you might find useful, such as books, websites or organizations.

We have set out to look at specific skills such as bike riding and soccer as well as giving ideas for other games and activities to do in order to support the development of physical skills as well as stamina and fitness.

It is intended that you will be able to use the activities and advice in a 'pick and mix' way, not necessarily in any order, but when your child expresses a desire to learn a new skill or activity. You could even use the book as a rainy day and holiday activity resource. The information in this book is not meant to be a therapeutic programme and is not a substitute for therapy intervention.

What is dyspraxia/developmental co-ordination disorder?

Dyspraxia is now commonly known as developmental co-ordination disorder, or DCD for short. (In this book we will use the term DCD.) It is not the purpose of the book to discuss the 'whys and wherefores' of DCD, as there are now many publications readily available. A list of publications is included in 'Further Reading' at the end of the book. However, as a backdrop to this book a summary of the 'condition' would be helpful.

What do we know about DCD? Current thinking is that it affects more boys than girls (with this in mind and for the ease of writing, we will be referring to 'him' and 'he' in the text as a generic term). As yet we do not know what causes it. It can affect children in a mild form or to such a significant degree that it gets in the way of everyday living and learning activities. Some children have difficulty with planning and organizing what they want to do and some children just don't seem to have the body mechanics to do the job. Others have a mixture of both. Up to 50 per cent of the more severely affected children will go on to experience some difficulties in adulthood. More often than not, DCD can overlap with other conditions such as dyslexia, attention deficit disorders and social communication disorders. Some children struggle to learn new skills and find the whole experience quite demoralizing, which can lead to a lack of confidence and motivation. This can sometimes be shown as difficult behaviour, being emotionally immature and having difficulty learning in school. At the moment there is not a cure. This makes the 'picture' of a child with DCD quite complicated. As a result, each child is different. Their own personality and other factors such as home life and culture can also have a bearing on how they cope with day-to-day life at home, play and school.

Some other areas of concern for parents/carers and professionals are the child's self-esteem, confidence and social skills. From experience it has been found that if this can be maintained, the children can cope better with some of the other things they find hard to do. This aspect will be considered in a bit more detail later on in the book.

Why do children with DCD experience difficulties with physical activities?

Children with DCD may experience problems with some or all of these aspects:

- *Technical*
  A variety of gross motor skills are required for sports and physical games. These may include physical elements such as balance, strength, speed, endurance, eye/hand or eye/foot co-ordination. Some children have difficulty recalling the correct response or sequence of actions or movements for a particular task. This is made harder for them if they have to react quickly and with precision.

- *Tactical*
  Difficulties with poor spatial/body awareness.

- *Language communication and social skills*
  Difficulties with understanding rules of games and following instructions. They may find it hard to articulate their point of view and get frustrated. Some children find it hard to make friends.

- *Psychological*
  Many children have insight into their difficulties. Depending on the nature of the child they may be able to laugh at themselves or they may lack confidence and be fearful of trying, especially if they have had a negative experience in the past. An example of this might be having to demonstrate a skill in a PE lesson in front of the whole class and doing it badly, therefore highlighting their difficulties to others. Often children with DCD can be emotionally immature, for example, moody/lose self-control, which will affect game playing.

Understandably when you find something hard it can be all too easy to give up quickly and therefore the child may seem to have poor concentration. They might be easily distracted or led by others. However, it must be stressed that some children have resilience – the ability to make sense and deal with problems on their own and make the best out of difficult situations.

It is especially important to offer your child reassurance and support when they need it because if they see that you are worried or frustrated it can affect their ability to cope even more.

- *Cognitive* (the mental processes of understanding, judgement, memory and reasoning, in other words, thinking) For some children their ability to make decisions may be poor or slow. Problem solving and strategy making can also be hard. Controlling the movements needed to perform a physical skill can take a lot of 'thinking energy', which does not leave much room to be creative. This skill is necessary for many activities in school and leisure activities. We can all remember PE lessons where we had to think of a way to move differently around the gym or move with a hoop or make a shape and balance! Everyone was standing and looking around for ideas from their classmates until someone made a start and you were able to get an idea from them. We can't all be the class trendsetter, but the creative juices just don't seem to flow for some children with co-ordination difficulties.

The need for physical fitness

Children with DCD are at risk of having lower levels of fitness than their peers because they find movement difficult. They are therefore less likely to participate fully in school PE lessons and even more unlikely to choose to take part in physical activities in their leisure time. This can lead to becoming less physically active and consequently less fit. Only one third of all children aged between 2 and 11 achieve the recommended one hour a day of moderate physical activity outside school hours. In Britain the time devoted to PE has reduced in recent years and in secondary schools there is less PE in England and

Wales than anywhere in the European Union. Adolescents are even less likely to choose to be physically active regardless of whether they have movement difficulties or not. Lower levels of physical activity together with high-calorie pop and snacks are largely responsible for the increase in obesity and diabetes in British children.

The recommended level of physical activity for children is an hour per day of moderate-intensity physical activity (enough to get your heart beating faster and break into a sweat). This need not be done all in one go and, in fact, the best way to achieve it is to consider healthy travel to school. Walking briskly or cycling is a great way to start the day both mentally and physically and at the end of the day is a great way to unwind your body and mind. (It keeps our planet healthy too!) Other forms of moderate intensity exercise are swimming, roller skating, skipping and mowing the lawn (this last one is great for staying healthy and getting pocket money!). It is also recommended that twice a week the activities should be more structured and designed to help improve bone health, muscle strength and flexibility: rebounding (jumping on the trampoline), skipping and roller skating, for example, or joining an activity class such as a martial art.

Besides improving healthy bodies, the right physical activity is great for improving self-esteem and can lead to becoming a physically active adult.

Parent/carer as a coach

In order to develop children's skills, they need to have opportunities to practise 'little and often'. It is important, however, that this is on a 'playful' basis and not 'workful' and therefore needs to be fun and motivating (no nagging allowed). The children need the support of 'another' as they cannot do it 'on their own'. This means that as a parent/carer you will have to 'play' too. This is not a bad thing...you will benefit from time spent with your child, being physically active and gaining a sense of being able to do something to help your child all at the same time. Marvellous!

Tips and hints

When helping your child to develop skills you will need to become the 'coach'. Here are some ideas about how to go about this:

- Play when you have time. 'A little and often' is best.

- Keep sessions short. It is better to do five minutes of top-quality activity rather than push for longer, causing you and your child to lose heart.

- Always check what your child has learned using a 'coaching technique'. Telling your child to bend his knees is not enough; he needs to understand why he is bending his knees in order to truly learn the skill.

Here is an example, which is about roller skating:

Adult: 'What is the skill we learned?'
Child: 'Basic position.'
Adult: 'And why do we do basic position?'
Child: 'So we are lower?'
Adult: 'Yes! Why would you want to be lower?'
Child: 'So that we have better balance? So that we make bigger pushes?'
Adult: 'Very good! And why would we want to make bigger pushes?'
Child: 'So we go faster!'

- Make sure the activities are appropriate to your child. It is important your child is not pushed too hard too soon. This may be difficult to gauge as your child might not be 'developmentally' ready for a skill although his friends may be. Work at your child's pace, not yours or their friend's.

- Supervision by an adult requires encouragement, reinforcement of good behaviour and feedback when appropriate. Be positive in your feedback. Praise all efforts – not just the end result.

- Get a balance between assisting and independence. It is often easy to take over and give too much help, which does not give your child the opportunity to learn through his own mistakes. Remember it is OK to make mistakes, so use the questioning technique described earlier. Some children find it useful if they use 'self-talk' (say out loud what they are doing) as this helps to reinforce learning. Also see the next section for other ideas.

- Children with DCD may get 'it' one day and then lose 'it' the next. Always recap and build up sequences to ensure confidence. There is always the danger of trying to do too much too soon. You may need to practise something for several days or weeks. Don't become too disheartened if something seems to take a long time to achieve. You may need to have a break from it for a short while and then go back to it.

- Mind your language! Give one instruction at a time. Try not to 'flower' what you say with too many words as your child is likely to become confused. Demonstrate wherever you can to reinforce what you are saying.

- Select activities that provide variety, and include challenges in each session, but ensure that they are 'doable'. Physical activity and enjoyment are the goals rather than proficiency or competition.

- Some children with DCD find it hard to maintain their stamina. They may take longer to get going but tire more quickly so they may need frequent breaks. They may have a poor response to heat and cold so you may need to be more selective about what activities you work on during the year.

- When children are laughing they are learning, so keep it fun.

If you don't have the patience to teach your child, then it may be better for someone else to do it, which will avoid any fisticuffs. Remember the old rule about never letting your partner teach you to drive!

Helping children to help themselves

So far, there has been a lot for you to think about and do. You may think this is a lot, but you will already do most of it without realizing it. However, it is important that the children are helped to think things through for themselves. Have you ever been in a situation, perhaps at work, where someone is showing you how to do something new and you say, 'Let me have a go, I can't do it like that, I need to find my own way'? The way you learned how to do something and then show your child may not be a way in which they like to learn. Research into the treatment for children with DCD suggests that getting the children to find solutions for themselves has a favourable outcome. We have called this approach 'Ready, Get Set, Go' and have adapted it for you to consider when working with your child (it can be used for homework and doing jobs around the house as well).

Ready, Get Set, Go

'Ready' – 'What do we need to do?'

'Get Set' – 'How are we going to do it?', 'What happens first?', 'What happens next?'

'Go' – Do it, have a go. As with all journeys, your child needs to ask 'Are we nearly there yet?' This gives an opportunity to consider how well they are doing and whether things need to be done differently to reach the end goal. In this case, go back to the 'Get Set' stage to work out what to do.

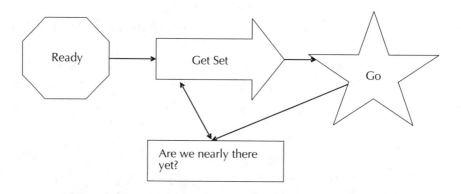

If your child forgets what to do, encourage him to think back to the steps he thought he needed. Try to ask questions, for example, 'What would happen if?', 'What could you do to make...happen?' or 'Can you think of another way?' This helps with reinforcing his own learning rather than 'Let me show you', 'You do it like this'.

Always revisit the 'ready' stage to help reinforce what he did well and where it went wrong; this helps him to reinforce the plan.

Of course, sometimes you will need to intervene as it is important to maintain your child's interest and motivation. Sometimes children will develop a technique that is not quite what you expected, but if it does the job...does it matter?

There is a useful website called 'dozlearn' referred to at the end of the Introduction, which offers lots of ideas on using visual prompters (pictures) to help with organization.

Maintaining interest

As we have already mentioned, it is important for all children to be physically active. There is much in the media at the moment regarding the merits of physical activity. However, what is known is that if you are not good at these types of things you will not want to expose yourself to them. The book aims to provide a number of ideas that can be used with other children or that they can do on their own. It is also important to remember that not all children particularly want to play team sports where they have to work as part of a team or in a more obvious competitive situation. This does not mean to say that they cannot be encouraged to know about the 'game'. Whilst they may not be actively involved, they still have the 'street cred' as they can talk about it with others and be part of the 'gang'.

Many children have a preference for and perform better at individual physical activities rather than team games or sports. There are many leisure activities and hobbies which can be played on a solitary basis, such as golf, or horse riding. See the Appendix for some suggestions which may be of interest to your child.

Joining clubs

For many children joining a sports club can be quite daunting. They may not know any of the other children or may feel nervous about not being as good as the others. This can be even more unnerving for children with movement problems who may have had a bad experience taking part in school PE lessons or playtimes. Being careful about the choice of activity will be important so as not to expose your child to potentially awkward situations.

Choose an activity that your child can do at their own pace and which has a reward scheme for achievement as this will be more motivating and provide a goal to encourage your child to keep going.

When you do find the right club, you need to consider the pros and cons of disclosing the nature of your child's difficulties.

- Find out what activity your child is interested in.
- What level of skill is required before joining the club? Some clubs set out to teach the basics of activities and the emphasis will be on skill acquisition and taking part, whereas others may be for more advanced players where they play to a high standard and the pressure to achieve success is great.
- Is the activity competitive? Is it a team activity where the pressure will be on not to 'let the team down' or where there are lots of rules and tactics to remember?

Table 1.1 Pros and cons of disclosing the nature of your child's difficulties

Pros	Cons
Speaking to the coach/organizer will enable him to make decisions about the amount of challenge he gives your child and the way he teaches new skills.	The coach/organizer may not want a child with different abilities in his team. He may not be willing to make allowances even though your child feels that they might be able to cope with a little extra help.
It will give the coach/organizer the chance to prepare activities in advance.	May make your child feel different and embarrassed.
To make sure the coach/organizer is aware of special points of importance such as not over stretching very mobile joints or to do longer warm-ups and cool downs to make allowances for lower muscle tone.	Your child may want to be treated the same as everyone else.
To make sure the coach/organizer is aware of any communication difficulties when giving instructions.	Other people or children may find out about your child's differences.

Using strengths

Sometimes it's hard to see past the 'can't dos'. Children with DCD have many strengths which can be utilized in game playing situations, such as strong oral skills, reading skills and imagination. It is important that, when participating in an activity, your child feels that they have a valuable contribution to make. This may mean thinking creatively about alternative roles with the same activity. For example, if they are a stickler for the rules let them be the referee.

Ready, Get Set, Go!

Well, now you are ready to have a go at some of the activities. We hope you find them useful and that you have lots of fun. There are just a few things to bear in mind though before you get started:

Safety disclaimer

Whilst every effort has been made to suggest games and activities which are safe for children, together with any precautions, there is no substitute for individual use of sound judgement. The activities in this book are suggestions, not recommendations. It is the reader's responsibility to use their own judgement and knowledge of safety when presenting activities. Children can be unpredictable, and close supervision is essential at all times. It would be sensible to make a brief 'risk assessment' before trying some of the activities. The writers accept no responsibility for damages resulting from the use of any activities included in this book.

Source disclaimer

It is in no way our intent to claim 'ownership' of these ideas. This manual is a collection of activities we have encountered or created ourselves over the years. It would be impossible to credit each activity, and thus we acknowledge that credit for this collection is shared among many persons. Where relevant, references are included at the end of each section.

Resource information

At the end of each chapter you will find helpful Resources and References sections. The details of suppliers are provided to give you a starting point for searching for and purchasing your own equipment, but although we have spoken to or purchased from some of them we are unable to make personal endorsements about any of them.

R ## Resources

do2learn: www.do2learn.com

References

Centre for Childhood Disability Research: www.canchild.ca

Drew, S. (2005) *Developmental Co-ordination Disorder in Adults*. Chichester: Whurr Publishers.

Games Development: www.gamesdevelopment.gaa.ie
    Provides information on Gaelic games.

Kirby, A. and Drew, S. (2003) *Guide to Dyspraxia and Developmental Co-ordination Disorders*. London: David Fulton Publishers.

National Heart Forum: www.heartforum.org.uk

Sustrans: www.sustrans.org.uk
    Provides information on cycling.

2 CAN'T PLAY WON'T PLAY

Making friends

Learning to make friends is one of the most significant tasks in a child's early social development. We can see from the Introduction that children with developmental co-ordination disorder (DCD) experience a number of challenges that impact on their ability to participate in play activities. Play is a really important job for children as it is through this medium that they learn many skills, not just from a physical perspective but also from a social and psychological perspective.

Where does it go wrong for children with DCD?

- Some, not all, children find it hard to 'read' people, situations or the expected behaviour in situations. Friendships may therefore be difficult, as the children find it hard to moderate their behaviour or to anticipate the results of their actions.

- They find it hard to understand and follow the rules of games so they may get angry easily and lose their temper when things don't go their way.

- They may have a poor sense of social distance.

- They may have difficulty regulating the tone and volume of their speech.

- Many of them may seem rather immature compared to their peers. As a result the children may tend to play with either younger or older children rather than their peers.

- At times they may seem to be obsessed with a limited range of play activities. This may be due to the fact they realize that they find things hard to do and have had limited positive experiences in some games. They therefore stick to simple and familiar games that they are comfortable with.

- Some children lack confidence and have low self-esteem, which makes them very shy and makes them feel uncomfortable and unsure of themselves around others.

- Sometimes they are ignored or teased by others because there is something 'different' about them that sets them apart from the other children.

? What can be done to help children develop friendships?

Different children have different needs when it comes to helping them get along better with others and making friends. For children with DCD we sometimes need to give extra help and support in learning the skills needed to make friends as well as by providing them with opportunities to interact with other children. It is easy to forget at what age children should be doing things because we can tend to think of them as 'little adults'. This can lead us to having higher expectations that they cannot attain.

Here are some ideas to help with making and keeping friends. However, it may also be necessary for you to work specifically on certain aspects of your child's social skills in order to ensure successful friendships. The following are considered to be some of the essential skills we need to be able to get on with and be accepted by others:

- greeting others
- listening and responding
- showing interest
- giving compliments
- understanding body language and tone of voice
- comprehending personal space
- joining ongoing activities with peers

- sharing and co-operating
- handling teasing
- managing anger.

Table 2.1 What's expected of children at various ages

Age	What's expected
3–4 years	Children are tuned into the 'here and now'. They define a friend as someone who happens to be near them or whose toys they like. They can be aggressive but want friends and enjoy being with other children. At this age they tend to brag and be bossy. They also need to feel important and worthwhile. They appreciate praise for their achievements.
5–6 years	Children focus on their own needs. They're beginning to realize that someone else may have a different point of view, but they don't realize that friendship is an ongoing process. They have a short-term view of friendship; it applies to episodes of being together.
7–9 years	Children realize that friendships are personal and they may like or dislike a person because of certain traits.
10 years	Children see friendships as an ongoing collaboration; they are able to take another person's point of view, share feelings, help each other and show interest in each other's activities, but they may exclude others. In the middle years of childhood children emerge as more independent social beings. Less reliant on the security of the family, they form ties with their peers.
12 years	Children recognize and value the complexity of human relationships.

Tips and hints

For children:

- Stand tall as you move around – practise in the mirror or with your mum or dad for a coach.
- Make eye contact and smile when someone looks at you.
- Hang around near a group that looks interesting.
- Decide what you want to say before you talk; don't just babble on.

- Catch the eye of someone in the group and smile. If that person smiles back, join in the group.
- Listen to the conversation and when you know what is going on, join in.
- Speak in a positive way and don't brag (boast).
- Join in with the group; don't try to take over.

Look for others who are alone or seem shy and introduce yourself. Ask them about their interests. You may turn out to have a lot in common.

Tips and hints

For parents with a young child:

- Children learn through imitating parents' behaviour. Think through your own experiences with friendships.
- Practise with your child by pretending to be different people in social situations (role playing). What would you do if...?
- Children need lots of real practice. Invite a few children over; set up play groups.
- Children are not likely to play easily until they know one another; start with easy activities to build friendships.
- Make sure your child has play experiences with children of different ages and backgrounds.
- Don't expect that younger children will have long-term relationships.
- Don't force sharing.
- Expect some conflict.
- Put a time limit on a game so it ends on success rather than failure.
- Present toys that children can use together.
- When you see conflict brewing, take a break for a story, song or juice.

Tips and hints

For parents with a school-aged child:

- Explain to your child about social distance – an elbow's width sitting next to someone, and an arm's length if he is standing in front of you, are simple measures you can teach.

- Check on eye contact – does he look at someone when he is talking to them at all or too much?

- Listen and accept your child's feelings no matter what they may be. Let your child know you're on their side.

- Examine your own feelings. Does the present conflict trigger off memories of some of your own early experiences?

- Expect some conflict. Children learn how to handle disagreements by having a few now and then. However, decide whether and to what degree you should get involved, for example, if there is quarrelling, see if they can work it out themselves. Try to be close by when there is a problem situation – do not intervene unless it becomes necessary.

- Help your child develop sharing and turn taking skills by using spinners or dice in games as well as other table top games such as cards or board games. Practise winning and losing.

- It is fine if your child has one or two good friends, rather than a large group of buddies.

- Have a quiet area where your child can go to be alone and regain control of their emotions (by choice).

- Encourage your child to talk about his feelings when others will not share or are rough.

- Use situation pictures and ask your child how he would solve the situation.

- Practise starting and ending a conversation with him. Pick a topic or hobby he enjoys. Think about a few topics that he can talk about in different social settings and let him practise it with you – for example, soccer, or a holiday he has been on.

- Practise good behaviour. Let your child practise with close family members who will be more lenient if mistakes are made. It must be agreed that they will not laugh at the child practising, otherwise any benefit will be dashed immediately, and make it harder to try again. They should not criticize him, but praise his efforts.

- To help develop your child's ability to 'read' emotions or body language, play a game of charades where each person has to act out a feeling, for example, anxious, happy or sad, then use this as an opportunity to talk about when and where you may feel like this.

Tips and hints

For parents with an adolescent:

- Set limits and ground rules.

- In family meetings, discuss critical issues such as curfews, money, allowance, family tasks, clothing and values in order to practise giving a point of view and listening to others.

- Encourage participation in new groups.

- Put 'popularity' in perspective. Some children prefer one or two close friends; others prefer larger groups.

- Respect your child's privacy.

- Encourage your child's positive efforts to get along with others, even when such attempts fail. Remind your child that making friends sometimes takes a long time, so it's important to keep trying. Ask questions and help him think about what the other child may need in a friend.

- Sometimes teenagers may need a bit of help getting a conversation started, so make it a point to be available, if you are needed. You don't want to hover and monopolize the conversation, but helping to oversee activities can give you the opportunity to keep things light.

'Practice makes perfect.' Make the time to play with your children; not only will it give you an idea about areas in which they may be struggling socially, but it gives them the chance to 'practise' their social skills. By your interacting with them, they will enjoy increased confidence in their ability to handle social situations. With little children, you can pretend to be in school, at the park or in a restaurant and switch roles with them, sometimes being the person who wants to make a new friend and sometimes being the person who is approached. These skills come naturally for some kids, but many children need a little help to understand how to make friends.

> If your child is being teased or bullied at school, talk to the teacher for assistance. All schools have a written policy for dealing with bullying. See the Resource section for information on bullying.

If your child gets a little frustrated try some of the relaxation games and ideas later on in the book.

Self-esteem

? *What is self-esteem?*

Self-esteem is the collection of beliefs or feelings that we have about ourselves, or our 'self-perceptions'. How we define ourselves influences our motivations, attitudes and behaviours and affects our emotional adjustment. Self-esteem develops from about four years to seven years of age. The child begins to make judgements about their physical and intellectual competence, social acceptance and behaviour. Early childhood experiences are therefore crucial in laying the foundations of future positive self-esteem. Healthy self-esteem is like having armour against the challenges of the world. Children who feel good about themselves seem to have an easier time handling conflicts and resisting negative pressures.

As children grow, their self-esteem fluctuates. It is frequently changed and fine-tuned because it is affected by their experiences and new perceptions. A child who has low self-esteem may not want to try new things. He may frequently speak negatively about himself, saying such things as, 'I'm stupid', 'I'll never learn how to do this' or 'What's the point, nobody cares about me anyway'. The child may exhibit a low tolerance for frustration, giving up easily or waiting for somebody else to take over.

It is possible to learn self-esteem, but it cannot be taught. In order to raise self-esteem we need to create an environment and provide experiences that will help the child to discover it for himself. Here are some general strategies that you might find helpful.

Tips and hints

- Support your child in learning that it is OK to make a mistake.

- Give hugs and encouragement and notice when your child is trying hard to succeed.

- Try not to compare differences between siblings and friends.

- Offer plenty of activities at which your child can succeed.

- Acknowledge feelings. Let children know it is OK to feel angry, alone, scared, or lonely. Give children the names for their feelings and words to express how they are feeling.

- Structure activities for co-operation, not competition. This allows individuals to work at their own pace and increases the learning of social skills.

- Laugh with your children and encourage them to laugh at themselves. People who take themselves very seriously are undoubtedly decreasing their enjoyment in life. A good sense of humour and the ability to make light of life are important ingredients for increasing one's overall enjoyment.

- Always reward good behaviour (achievements in activities and behaviour itself) with praise and positive feedback. This helps your child internalize the sense of success and having a valid role, which in turn improves self-esteem.

Making friends, social skills and self-esteem for children with DCD is a significant area of concern for parents and carers. The topic in itself warrants a book of its own. However, there are lots of resources which can provide useful information to help you support your child in this area. Listed below are just some of the sources that we have found.

From our experience many of the children we have met feel that they are the only ones who find it hard to make friends and play games with ease. We have found that by meeting other children who experience similar difficulties their confidence begins to grow. Most areas now have a support group and often activities and clubs for the children. Contact the Dyspraxia Foundation to see if there is one in your locality.

R Resources

Family support organizations

Australian Dyspraxia Association (ADA) Inc: www.dyspraxia.com.au

Bullying online: www.bullying.co.uk

Child Welfare League of America: www.cwla.org
> An association of public and private nonprofit agencies that assist abused and neglected children and their families with a wide range of services.

Children Now: www.childrennow.org
> A nonpartisan, independent voice for children, working to translate the nation's commitment to children and families into action. Utilizes research and mass communications to make the well-being of children a top priority across the nation.

Children's Defense Fund: www.childrensdefense.org
> Provides a strong, effective voice for the children of America, who cannot vote, lobby or speak for themselves.

Children's Trust Fund, 294 Washington Street, Suite 640, Boston, MA 02108; Telephone: +1 (617) 727 8957; Fax: +1 (617) 727 8997

Christine Meredith, Can-Do Cottage, 82 Cox Street, South Windsor, NSW 2756, Australia; Postal address: PO Box 5519, South Windsor, NSW 2756, Australia; Telephone: +61 (0) 24577 6220; Email: information@dyspraxia.com.au

Connect for Kids: www.connectforkids.org
> An award-winning multimedia project of the Benton Foundation; helps adults make their communities better places for families and children.

Contact a Family: www.cafamily.org.uk
> A charity for families with disabled children.

Dyscovery Centre: www.dyscovery.co.uk
 Helping individuals with learning difficulties.

Dyspraxia Foundation: www.dyspraxiafoundation.org.uk

Dyspraxic Teens Forum: www.dyspraxicteens.org.uk

Early Childhood Australia National Office: www.earlychildhood.org.au
 Email: eca@earlychildhood.org.au
 Responsible for the overall co-ordination of Early Childhood Australia's
 nationwide advocacy role for young children and publications programme.

Family Support America: www.familysupportamerica.org
 Formerly Family Resource Coalition of America; provides information on
 publications, curricula, conferences and more.

Growing Kids: www.growingkids.org
 Tips and advice.

Kidscape: www.kidscape.org.uk
 A charity established to prevent bullying and child abuse.

Matts Hideout: www.matts-hideout.co.uk
 Information about hidden disabilities, bullying and home education.

MELD (Parents as Teachers): www.parentsasteachers.org
 Provides resources and information for parents and providers. MELD's
 mission is to enhance the capacity of those who parent to raise nurtured,
 competent children.

Shykids: www.shykids.com

YoungMinds: www.youngminds.org.uk
 A charity committed to improving the mental health of all children and
 young people.

Social skills

Also see products and books below.

Feel Good Friends: www.feelgoodfriends.com

Special Education:
 www.specialed.about.com/cs/behaviordisorders/a/social.htm

Products and books

Biggs, V. (2005) Caged in Chaos: A Dyspraxic Guide to Breaking Free.
 London: Jessica Kingsley Publishers.

Boon, M. (2000) Helping Children with Dyspraxia. London: Jessica Kingsley
 Publishers.

Drew, S. (2003) Jack and the Disorganised Dragon. Cardiff: Dyscovery Press.
 (A story for children, available from www.dyscovery.co.uk)

Jessica Kingsley Publishers: www.jkp.com

Lucky Duck Publishing: www.luckyduck.co.uk

Macintyre, C. (2000) *Dyspraxia in the Early Years: Identifying and Supporting Children with Movement Difficulties*. London: David Fulton Publishers.

Portwood, M. and O'Neil, J. (1999) *Developmental Dyspraxia: Identification and Intervention: A Manual for Parents and Professionals*. London: David Fulton Publishers.

Reed, J. (2005) *Things that Go Bump in the Day: A Story about a Boy with Coordination Difficulties* (available from www.therapybookshop.com)

Scholastic: www.scholastic.co.uk

Special Direct: www.specialdirect.com (UK)
Telephone: 0800 318 686

References

Ayres, J. (1987) *Sensory Integration and the Child*. Los Angeles: Western Psychological Services.

Canadian Child Care Federation: www.cccf-fcsge.ca

Fast-Track (n.d.) 'Why Children Have Trouble Making Friends.' Duke University/Pennsylvania State University/University of Washington/Vanderbilt University. Accessed on 16/08/07 at www.childandfamilypolicy.duke.edu/fasttrack/parents.html

Fishaut, E. (2005) 'Making Friends.' Minnesota: University of Minnesota. Accessed on 16/08/07 at www.extension.umn.edu/info-u/families/BE907.html

KidSource Online: www.kidsource.com

Kirby, A. (1999) *Dyspraxia: The Hidden Handicap*. London: Souvenir Press.

Kirby, A. and Drew, S. (2003) *Guide to Dyspraxia and Developmental Co-ordination Disorders*. London: David Fulton Publishers.

OT Works: www.otworks.ca
Canada's occupational therapy research site.

3 LET'S GO SWIMMING

In this chapter, we will be considering one of the best ways to get fit, socialize, improve strength, fitness and co-ordination and give your child a fighting chance if ever he gets into difficulties in our waterways or pools.

Swimming develops many skills:

- balance
- co-ordination
- body awareness and spatial awareness
- whole body strength
- flexibility
- physical fitness
- social skills
- activities of daily living like dressing and personal hygiene.

Before you start, it is worth bearing in mind some concerns that other parents and carers have mentioned to us in the past and we will provide you with the advice we gave them to help (truly tried and tested!). It is worth remembering for this activity that the emphasis is not on swimming or stroke technique, but more about being water confident and having fun.

Once your child is water confident, he will be able to join swimming classes and clubs. This can open the door to other aquatic sports such as speed swimming, water polo, canoeing, body boarding and sub-aqua diving. 'The world's your ocean' as they say!

You will be aware of your child's difficulties learning new skills, co-ordinating movement, having little stamina and stability and being disorganized. In the swimming pool his body becomes like a lead weight (he's better under water than on it and can't seem to balance in the water in order to make use of his arms and legs). However, you will be relieved and thrilled to know that swimming is one of the skills which, given the right amount of help, can be mastered and your child can be successful at. This helps improve his self-esteem and confidence no end!

Notes for grown-ups

If *you* aren't confident in water yourself, then your apprehension can be sensed by your child which can cause him to be unsettled. It's worth spending time in a pool without your child first or even taking some swimming lessons yourself. You may enjoy the experience, get fitter, lose weight and find a new hobby. *Every cloud has a silver lining*!

? Where does it go wrong?...those frustrating times
Before you get into the pool

You should remember that this may be a difficult or stressful occasion for your child, so don't be disappointed if he won't go in the first time. Avoid trying to embarrass him by comparing him unfavourably with other children.

Many parents tell us that they have experienced some of the following problems before getting to the pool:

- remembering swimming kit (or underwear if already changed into costume)
- undressing
- getting into the water (slippery pool sides and not wanting to expose his body)
- understanding the rules of the pool including consequences of risky behaviour
- noise levels and quality of sounds that may be too frightening for those children with sensitive hearing (may also affect balance)

- needing a token or coin to use the lockers (and you're not in the same changing room as your child!)
- the child cannot cope in group swimming lessons.

Tips and hints

- Children with organization and planning difficulties find it hard to learn the art of making lists, which those of us who are parents will have learned as we grew up. Before going to the pool, help your child with planning what to do and what to take. Help to draw up a list – this can be in pictures (see Resources for a useful visual strategies website) – take photographs or write it down. Here's an example list:
    - underwear
    - goggles
    - arm bands
    - towel
    - shampoo
    - locker token or coin.
- Suggest your child gets changed into his swimwear before he goes to save time but remind him to pack his underwear.
- Suggest your child wears easy/loose fitting clothes to help with undressing and then dressing after the swim.
- Buy a charity coin token which can be clipped on to the swimming bag and then used to access the locker. Don't forget to take it out again afterwards.
- Many boys' trunks are tied at the waist, so look for some which are elasticated.
- If your child's balance is poor then make sure he sits down to get changed. The slippery floor will only make it harder for him. Encourage your child to fold his clothes as he takes them off then put them in a pile. This will mean that they are in the right order to go back on afterwards.
- Some children find the noise and bustle of the pool overwhelming and sometimes overstimulating. Find out when the pool is less busy; keep them in a quieter corner of the

pool, facing away from the centre and try using earplugs to dim the noise.

- The poolside can be unnerving as it is slippery to walk on, so give your child non-slip waterproof shoes to wear until you reach the edge of the pool.
- If your child is self-conscious about his body, wearing a swimming robe, T-shirt or tracksuit top to the water will help as a cover up.
- If your child can't cope in group swimming lessons, consider asking the local swimming instructor if he or she will do private lessons. It may help if you explain that your child is unable to cope in group situations.

In the pool

These are some of the difficulties that we have experienced with our children:

- fearful of the depth of the water or not appreciating the changes in depth throughout the pool
- lacking water confidence and hating getting the face near the water or splashed
- chlorine makes eyes sore – to wear or not wear goggles?
- can't float
- can't co-ordinate arms with legs
- getting cold too quickly.

Tips and hints

- Although many swimming instructors prefer children to use the steps to enter and leave the pool, it is important that they learn to enter and leave the water from the poolside too. Sit on the side of the pool with your child's feet resting on the trough if there is one. The adult stands in front, already in the water. Encourage your child to put both hands together on to the poolside beside his hip, then roll over towards this side on to his front (tummy). Next, he should slide down into the water feet first ending up in the water, feet on the pool bottom, resting the hands on the trough or handrail (getting out again is discussed later). This way the steps are not used and the upper body will be strengthened at the same time. It will also give a better chance of getting out from a pool away from steps or from the sea or riverbank, for example.

- Children who have poor body and spatial awareness (sense of where their body is in space or where their arms and legs are in relation to their body) can find themselves at a loss when their body is under the surface of the water. Ask the pool management whether they will allow wetsuits in the pool or try buying a full Lycra body suit which when wet will give a tight fit around the limbs and increase body awareness.

- Give your child goggles if necessary to prevent chlorine stinging the eyes. They can sometimes make the difference between getting the face near the water and not. However, if your child is particularly nervous in the water, it is wiser not to use goggles so that you can see your child's eyes and levels of attention. It is possible to buy over-the-counter eye drops to relieve the stinging from the pool water, but speak to your pharmacist about this next time you go to the chemist.

- Teach your child where to look for the depth indicators on the poolside and also give him 'environmental cues' such as 'Don't go past the lifeguard's station or chair'.

- Make a mental list of the things you want to achieve in the water to reduce the amount of time hanging around. Keep a tracksuit top or towel on poolside. You might also take our suggestions with you, which can be photocopied and laminated to make them waterproof. If your child complains of feeling cold in the water, do some more physical activities like silly walks or jumping in the water to warm up again.

- Take small floating toys with you to maintain your child's interest and attention in the pool (see photograph later in the chapter).

- Your child may find it difficult to concentrate on instructions in a group situation as he cannot filter out the words from all the background noise. Keep the instructions short and repeat them and give a demonstration if possible. Ask your child to repeat them back to you (this may be the reason why group swimming lessons in the past have been unsuccessful).

Getting out and going home again

Some common problems are:

- climbing out of the water
- getting showered and shampooed
- getting dry
- getting dressed
- doing it all on his own because there are no family changing facilities available.

Tips and hints

- When getting out of the water, encourage your child to place both his hands on to the poolside. To build up momentum, he should jump up and down three times as if to push out of the pool. On the fourth jump, he should push harder on the hands and jump higher and land his tummy on the poolside. Then he can roll or wriggle further away from the poolside and sit up safely on the edge. Stand behind your child just in case, but offer little or no assistance. By leaving the water in this way he will build up upper body strength and it will help if you are anywhere where there are no steps.

- Your child should wear non-slip shoes to leave the poolside and to provide some stability once in the shower as soapy water and ceramic tiles are extremely slippery. If available or necessary, use the disabled shower unit where you will find a shower-chair.

- Use 'all-in-one' shampoo and conditioner to minimize the number of bottles you need to have in the shower (for long hair, you can use detangling spray once dressed).

- It's easier to remove swimming costumes (especially all-in-one suits) in the shower but if they are communal showers this may not be possible. Take a robe or towel with you to walk back with. If you don't have a towel robe and are good with a needle and thread, sew two towels together down the sides, leaving space for head and arms (like a tabard). Some children actually prefer to get changed inside these rather than expose themselves in communal changing areas.

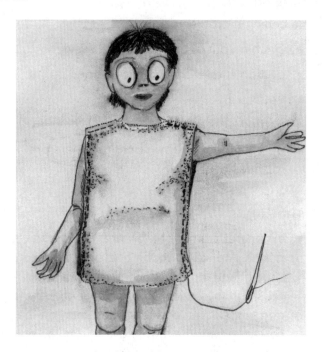

- When dressing after the swim, use talcum powder (provided that your child isn't sensitive to talc) to make putting the clothes back on easier.

A word on flotation aids

Using arm bands: These are useful for safety and making your child feel more at ease whilst allowing some freedom of movement and separation from you. The disadvantages are that children can become reliant on them and then become reluctant to take them off again. Some children may become overconfident when wearing them and be tempted to swim off to deeper waters. Some experts advise not to use them at all. The best type to buy is those that comply with National Safety Standards, which are inflatable and have a double chamber (if one half pops or deflates, the other chamber stays inflated, giving some support).

Aquapacks: These are inflatable packs which strap to the child's back. The pressure of the water can force the pack up around the neck and they can tend to make the child swim more upright in the water.

Floats: Polystyrene floats are easily available and useful for encouraging a flatter body position in the water for swimming.

Float swimwear: There are a variety of swimsuits available. The float system is integrated into the costume, making it more streamlined and easier to move about in (see the Resources section for suppliers).

Getting into the water and having fun

The following ideas suggest some games to play in the water with your child. Remember that this is about having fun and stroke style is not important.

Activities for water confidence

Learning to put the face into the water is an important skill but even more important is learning to blow out through the mouth whenever the face is near the water. This skill will prevent breathing in water and choking.

- Play at washing hands and face in the water.
- Blow the water away from the face. This is the most basic skill for swimming. Take a table tennis ball or 'Fried Egg' toy (see Resources) and get your child to blow it away from them. Holding on to your child's hands, place the floating toy between you and in between your child's arms. Get your child to walk forwards across the width of the pool blowing the toy in front of him (you should be walking backwards).
- Drop down so that the shoulders are under the water. Practise the blowing activity above, keeping low to the water.
- As the confidence grows, ask your child to put their face into the water and blow the toy with the mouth just in the water to blow bubbles.
- Go back to the side of the pool and holding the rail with both hands, jump up and down so that the water is above the shoulders. If it is easier, jump up and down until the face is in the water and so on until the whole head is under the water – come back up for air of course!

- Stand in the water just above the waist. Start by just walking across the pool sliding the feet along the floor. Go back to the side and this time try running across or pretending to be a kangaroo by jumping across. (You can walk in front of your child with palm to palm grip here until they are confident enough without touching then progress to doing it with you walking to the side of them.)

- Play push and glide from the rail (lie on tummy and push off from the wall with the feet). Practise this lying face down and if your child is confident enough, on the back.

- In the shallow end of the water lie out straight in the water, pushing up through the arms, and walk along using the hands for feet. If your child is confident enough play the same game, but on the back. This activity is great if your pool has a 'shore line' or gradual slope into the water.

The painting game
WHAT YOU NEED
Nothing

WHAT YOU DO
This poolside activity is great for children under five who are non-swimmers or who may be fearful of water. Gather the players

along the side of the pool and ask them each to pick their favourite colour. Then, pretending their arm is a brush and the pool is a big can of their colour paint, have them bend over, 'stir' the paint and coat a part of their body. Then they choose another colour and cover another part of their body. Repeat this until the players have painted themselves everywhere including their face and hair. When they're all painted, they can either jump to a waiting adult in the pool for a 'wash' or, if they're nervous, just pretend to shower themselves with water scooped in their hands. This helps the children to get comfortable with water getting on various parts of their bodies.

Motor boat

WHAT YOU NEED
Nothing

WHAT YOU DO
Here's a singing game that helps young children get over their fear of the water. Hold your child under the arms in the water facing you and at eye-level with you (you may have to crouch down). Then, pulling your child in a circle through the water, sing or chant, 'Motor boat, motor boat, go so slow,' while your child blows bubbles or kicks his feet. Then increase the speed, if your child is OK with that, and sing, 'Motor boat, motor boat, go so fast. Motor boat, motor boat, step on the gas!' And go as fast as your child likes. This game not only gets your child to feel comfortable while face down in the water, but it also teaches blowing out – not to suck water in. It also introduces the idea of kicking. Next play the game again with your child on his back.

Games to play

The following games are great to play if there are a few of you. They are great for the whole family or friends to get involved with. Some of them are less active than others; the key shows the degree of skill required.

Easy (E): useful for early water confidence.

Medium (M): some swimming ability and not afraid to get head under the water.

Harder (H): also needs floating skills, some swimming skills and confidence to lie back in the water unaided.

Electricity (E)
WHAT YOU NEED
Three or more players

WHAT YOU DO
Stand in a circle holding hands. One player 'switches on' the current by squeezing the hand of the person next to him. The person whose hand is squeezed ducks under the water and comes back up again, then squeezes the next person's hand. This continues round the circle. You all end up 'bobbing up and down' in the water.

Lumberjack (M)
WHAT YOU NEED
Any number of players

WHAT YOU DO
This activity will help children who are more confident at entering the water and is a nice game to play if there are several swimmers. Get out of the water and stand close to the edge of the pool and pretend to be trees. Then get one child to be the lumberjack who comes to 'cut' down the trees. As each tree is cut down (by tapping the tree lightly), a child jumps (no diving!) into the water. Gradually move from shallow to deeper water as the 'trees' get confident.

Wheelbarrow race (M)
WHAT YOU NEED
Two or more pairs

WHAT YOU DO
One partner supports the other's legs and pushes him forward. The 'wheelbarrow' can either swim with his arms or keep them outstretched.

Still pond (H)
WHAT YOU NEED
Three or more players

WHAT YOU DO
Everyone floats as still as possible while one person watches. The last one to move is the winner.

Tunnel swim (H)

WHAT YOU NEED

Two or more pairs

WHAT YOU DO

Split into two 'teams'. Each team stands in line, one player in front of the other, legs apart. The person at the back of each team swims through the team's legs and stands up at the front. The next person then sets off and so on, until all the team has swum through.

Pair swim (H)

WHAT YOU NEED

Two or more pairs

WHAT YOU DO

Each pair links arms, then pushes off from the side and swims an agreed distance together. One child uses the right arm to make one side of the stroke, whilst the other child uses the left arm.

Chain swim (H)

WHAT YOU NEED

Two or more pairs

WHAT YOU DO

Divide into two teams and swim joined up, lightly holding the ankles of the person in front.

Chasing games

Sharks and minnows (E)

WHAT YOU NEED

Three or more players

WHAT YOU DO

One person is the shark and stands in the middle of the pool. The others are minnows and line up at one side. When the shark shouts 'sharks and minnows', they have to try and reach the other side without being caught. As soon as someone is caught, he changes into a shark and helps to catch the remaining minnows. Last one to be caught becomes the shark next game.

What time is it, Mr Shark? (E)

WHAT YOU NEED
Three or more players

WHAT YOU DO
The shark stands at one side of the pool, hands over his eyes, back to the other players, who line up on the other side. They shout 'What time is it, Mr Shark?', he replies, for example, 'Five o'clock', and they can then take five paces forward. The aim is to reach and touch the other side, but when the shark thinks they're getting close he suddenly shouts 'Dinner time', turns round and chases them. If he catches someone before they get back to their own side, they become Mr Shark.

Red letter (E)

WHAT YOU NEED
Three or more players

WHAT YOU DO
'It' stands at one side of the pool, hands over his eyes, back to the other players, who line up on the other side. 'It' calls out letters of the alphabet: whenever he calls a letter that is in a player's name, that player can take a step forward. The aim is to reach and touch the other side but when they are getting close, 'It' suddenly shouts 'Red letter', turns round and chases them. If someone is caught before they get back to their own side, they become 'It'.

Simon says (E)

WHAT YOU NEED
Two players or more

WHAT YOU DO
One person gives commands and the others have to do what he says, for example:

'Simon says jump!' – players have to jump

'Simon says leap into water!' – players have to leap into water

'Simon says swim front crawl!' – players have to swim front crawl

'Simon says get an inflatable and swim around for a minute'...

Do these in any order and make up your own as well.

Scavenger hunt (M)
WHAT YOU NEED
Two or more players; pool toys or any other items that sink

WHAT YOU DO
Strew a variety of items at the bottom of the pool: dive rings, spoon, coins, anything that doesn't float, isn't made of glass and has no sharp edges. Make sure there are two of everything (one for each team). The team collects the items in a certain amount of time.

Dolphin relay (M)
WHAT YOU NEED
Two or more players; balls

WHAT YOU DO
You will need a big ball each for this game. Divide into 'teams'. Each player moves across the pool in whatever way they can with confidence (this could be swimming or walking) whilst pushing the ball with their noses and forehead. If they touch the ball with their hands or any other part of their body they must go back to where that took place and start again. An easier way to do this is to make waves with the hands to 'push' the ball across the pool.

Log roll tag (H)
WHAT YOU NEED
Three or more players

WHAT YOU DO
'It' sculls or floats on his back while the others move round him in a circle, trying to get as close as possible. He suddenly rolls over and tries to catch someone. When someone is caught, they become 'It'.

Ideas for small toys/equipment for use in the pool
Many swimming pools have a range of floating toys and activities to use in the water which you may have access to. If you take a net bag with your own toys you should ask the pool manager if it is OK to use them.

There are a number of great pool (and bath) toys available nowadays which act as great motivators when playing in the water. Most can be bought from commercial retailers. Here are just a few to give you some ideas. Check out our Resources section for suppliers.

Noodles: These are made of soft, flexible foam and are about two metres long. They can be used as a flotation aid, splashing with, making waves, exercising or riding like a sea horse.

Things that sink: There are readily available sinking rings, hoops and sticks but you can make a fun garden from plastic flowers weighted down with plasticine!

Things that float: Corks, ping pong balls, inflated rubber gloves, small empty pop bottles, sponges (but you have to be quick before they sink!) and bath toys.

Throwing and catching objects: Inflatable beach balls move quite quickly in the pool and across the water but are easy to pack up flat to transport to and from the pool. Balls that will sit on the water or absorb water may be harder to throw (which is good for arm strength) but don't move as far or as quickly on the surface of the water. Remember that throwing and catching in the pool will also help with ball skills for PE and games.

Moving on

You've been there and done that, you've even bought the T-shirt. Well done! It may have taken a huge amount of effort for you and your child but the rewards will be clear to see. You will have helped your child to help himself, which when growing towards young adulthood is a really important skill.

R ## Resources

Books

Meredith, S. (2006) *Teach Your Child to Swim*. London: Usborne.

Swimming pool toys/equipment

Davies Sports: www.daviessports.co.uk (UK)
    Telephone: +44 (0) 845 120 4515

FloatSuit International: www.floatsuitinternational.com (US)

Paul's Warehouse: www.paulswarehouse.com.au

Pool Toy: www.pooltoy.com (US)

Pool Toys: www.bcl.com.au/shop/toys-pool.htm

Swim Outlet: www.swimoutlet.com (US)

Swim Ways: www.iqkids.com/swimways.html (US)

Visual Strategies: www.do2learn.com/picturecards/printcards/index.htm

Yardgames: www.yardgames.com.au

Young Minds: www.youngminds.com.au/catalog (educational toys)

Swimming organizations

Check out local leisure centres which may offer more specialized swim sessions for children with a range of disabilities.

Aquatic Therapy and Rehab Institute: www.atri.org (US)
    Telephone: +1 (866) go2-ATRI (+1 (866) 462 2874); Email: atri@atri.org
    The leading source of multidisciplinary aquatic therapy education.

Disability Sport England: www.disabilitysport.org.uk

Disability Sport Northern Ireland: www.dsni.co.uk

Disability Sport Scotland: www.scottishdisabilitysport.com

Disability Sport Wales: www.fdsw.org.uk

Halliwick Association of Swimming Therapy: www.halliwick.org.uk
    ADKC Centre, Whitstable House, Silchester Road, London W10 6SB;
    Telephone: +44 (0) 20 8968 7609
    Teaches water confidence and control of the body in the water, leading

towards swimming movements. When the basic skills have been mastered, more traditional swimming/stroke technique lessons can follow.

National Association of Swimming Clubs for the Disabled: www.nasch.org.uk c/o Rosemary O'Leary, The Willows, Mayles Lane, Wickham, Hants PO17 5ND; Telephone: +44 (0) 1329 833689

References

Fun and Games: www.funandgames.org

Fun-Attic: www.funattic.com (US)

RoSPA:
www.rospa.com/waterandleisuresafety/factsheets/children_swimming.htm

4 ON YOUR BIKE!

Teaching your child to ride a bike is one of those special times which, for many parents, is a mix of frustration, sore muscles, complete joy and total pride as you see the back of your child cycling away from you. Unfortunately, for parents and carers of children with co-ordination difficulties this can be a very frustrating time. It often takes much longer to gain the movement skills and confidence to balance and steer their bike. Many children become distressed and unhappy and will reject the bike altogether. However, the good news is that most children who find these skills hard to master actually do learn to ride a bike eventually and have many years of pleasure and physical activity from cycling.

Cycling develops many skills:

- balance

- co-ordination

- multi-tasking (doing more than one thing at a time!)

- it can be a social activity with family and friends

- it can enable your child to join a cycling club in a Veladrome (indoor or outdoor cycle track with curved sides) or a road riding club, to go mountain biking and to have an alternative means of transport for getting to and from school or a friend's house. Later they may even cycle to work

- road safety. Children should also learn road safety as they develop their skills on the bike which will help them as pedestrians or later on, drivers. It is another of those life skills which can open opportunities for your child and is a cheap form of physical activity that can be performed throughout their life.

In this chapter we will let you in on some tricks of the trade to help speed up the learning process and lessen the frustration and sense of failure.

? When should you start?

Children start learning the skills they will need to ride a bike quite early on, first by learning to crawl and walk, to balance in sitting, make the two sides of the body and top and bottom halves of the body work together. Later they will use a sit and ride toy by pushing with their feet and then pedal a tricycle to develop the strength and co-ordination they will need. If your child was late mastering any of these skills, then he may well be late learning to ride a bike even though he may want to because his friends are doing the same thing. Surprisingly, many parents have told us that despite not mastering other simple skills, their child has learnt to ride a bike through grim determination because it's what his friends are doing! For most children, this will happen at between seven and nine years of age, but we've all seen amazing tiny tots bombing around the local park. Don't be disheartened, they are the exception to the rule!

If your child can balance on one leg, hop and skip, he will have the necessary ingredients needed to start. Being able to steer and use the brakes takes concentration, co-ordination and strength, but these skills will develop as your child learns to control his bike.

To begin with, learning to ride a bike is a 'fair-weather activity'. It's hard enough without getting cold and wet at the same time. Late spring school holidays or summer school breaks are good times as they offer a longer period of time for lots of short duration practices. 'Little and often' is a good motto.

Notes for grown-ups
It is important to discuss safety issues with your child before they even get on their bike.

Before your child gets on the bike
Tips and hints

It's important to consider clothing at this point. For example, tight fitting fabrics will stop garments rubbing the skin.

- *Trousers*: It would be tempting to put your child in long trousers to protect their knees from all the tumbles but, unless they fit tightly around the ankles and lower legs, they can get caught in the bike chain or wheel and cause an injury. Bicycle clips are *so* 'last century' but do a good job when the trouser legs are wrapped around the leg first and then applied over the top. Horse riding suppliers sell lower leg 'chaps' or 'gaiters', which are elasticated, slightly padded leg protectors made to wear over slim trousers (see the Resources section).

- *Skirts*: These are a nightmare because they flap about or ride up and cause a loss of concentration when modesty prevails. Just 'steer' clear of these!

- *Tights*: When worn under sports shorts, tights are another good option to protect the legs from the weather, and also minor grazes. They keep the muscles warm. They are also cheaper than buying expensive cycle shorts even if these do have a padded bottom.

- *Tops*: These should have long sleeves to protect from grazes to elbows, offer warmth to muscles but allow the skin to breathe.

- *Shoes*: Velcro-fastening shoes are best as they hold closely on to the feet and don't have any dangly bits which might get caught. Make sure shoes with laces have them tucked firmly inside so as not to catch in the bike chain. Shoes with a big heel are also a big 'no no'. Trainers are very good as they give good traction (sticking power) for the feet on the pedals and, when the feet are on the ground more than the pedals, give good foot and ankle stability.

- *Gloves*: These will help protect the hands against grazing but proper cycling gloves can be bought very cheaply these days, even from your supermarket. They are padded, fingerless gloves which allow your child to 'feel' the handles/brakes but improve grip on them at the same time. As an additional protection, *skate pads* can be worn to protect knees and elbows further. They may also give the really timid rider a bit more confidence.

The cycle helmet
- The *cycle helmet* is the most important article of clothing when riding a bike and it should be *worn at all times* when using bikes.
- Helmets can be purchased from your local supermarket, bike shop or, in some places, the local Road Safety Centre.
- Make sure the helmet fits properly. Bike shops and the Road Safety Centre will help make sure the helmet is fitted properly for your child at no extra expense.
- If there is no one to help you with the correct fit of the helmet for your child, make sure the helmet is a snug fit and sits on top of the head not tipped back.
- If the worst happens and your child has a fall, or even if the helmet is hit – when it's thrown under the stairs, for example – it *must* be replaced as it will no longer protect your child's head.
- Make sure the children know how to put the helmet on correctly and learn how to fasten it and tighten the chin strap as well as releasing the clasp.

A bike helmet reduces the risk of serious brain injury by 88 per cent. 'No helmet, No bike.'

Training wheels or no training wheels, that is the question

Opinion is divided on this issue. Some people feel that using training wheels makes it take longer to ride independently because children can become dependent on them. For children with co-ordination difficulties, the need to balance, steer and co-ordinate movements all at the same time is an impossible task. Removing one of the skills and allowing the child to concentrate on pedalling and steering, for example, can help reduce stress and improve the speed of learning. Training wheels can be adjusted to sit on the ground or later on, as skills develop, can be raised by 1 cm (0.5 inches) off the ground. This gives a sense of freedom yet gives support during the wobbly bits. If both training wheels can touch the ground at once, there is little weight on the bicycle's rear wheel. This can reduce connection with the ground and reduce breaking power to zero. On uneven ground, the child may get stuck because the wheel spins.

For the older child whose bike does not come equipped with training wheels, some cycle suppliers offer a range of training wheels to suit larger-wheeled bikes, but these are still fairly limited.

By removing the pedals, your child can concentrate on learning to steer and balance on the bike. When they can 'freewheel' with their feet off the floor, you will know they are ready to add the pedalling skill! There are companies who sell special two-wheeled bikes which do not have pedals on them, but many are costly and you will still have to buy a 'proper' bike once your child gets to the 'freewheeling' stage. Much cheaper to take off the pedals, but remember where you put them and make sure all the screws go back on!

Instead of removing the need to pedal the bike, you can reduce the need to balance and steer by using an 'add on' bike. A 'tag-a-long' or trailer bike attaches to the seat pillar of an adult bike so that an older child (four to nine years) can be towed. The trailer bike consists of a normal child's cycle but without a front wheel or any steering mechanism. The child can pedal or freewheel independently of the towing adult. Some models may feature brakes or gears for the child (see the Resources section for suppliers).

Location, location, location

Choose flat ground, usually pavement and, if possible, in a park away from traffic. You will need lots of open space so that when your child gets going he doesn't need to stop or swerve to miss other people or obstacles. Somewhere with nice soft grass verges would also be great in case of falls.

Speaking of falls...

Reassure your child that this will happen and is quite normal. Their clothes should offer some protection but they should learn not to brace (tense) their joints when they fall.

The bike itself

Your local bike shop will help you measure the frame to suit your child. In fact, it is always best to buy your bike from a recognized dealer as they do come in bits and will require assembling at home. (This is a nightmare on Christmas Eve!) Your dealer can arrange to assemble the bike for you and make sure all the relevant bits are present, correct and tightened (they may need a day or two's notice and sometimes make a small charge). They can also make last-minute adjustments to the size of the bike to make a snug fit for your child. Ideally, your child should be able to stand on the balls of their feet (not the toes) when sitting on the saddle. Make sure that the frame (not the wheel height) is correct before purchase. As mentioned, your child should be able to touch the floor with the balls of both feet when sitting on the saddle but, if the frame is too high, he might hurt himself on the cross bar if he stops suddenly and slides forwards.

If you are buying the bike as a present then it would help the bike dealer to know your child's height and inside leg measurement.

- *The seat position* should be slightly lower when starting off to give greater comfort and confidence. The saddle should be positioned horizontally, that is, front and back of saddle at the same height.

- *The handlebar position* is better in a higher position when starting to learn so that your child is in a more upright position and can see straight ahead of him without having to move the head up or down too much.

From the age of nine onwards, children are starting to be more adventurous and pushing for independence. This is also the time when they learn to make better judgements about road safety and being near traffic. However, there are far more cars and lorries on the roads these days and despite many town planning departments painting cycle lanes on the roads cyclists are still very vulnerable to collision.

Remember the 'Green Cross Code'?

Research in Canada and America found that learning about 'in-car safety' and road safety before your child learns to ride a bike will be more likely to prevent an accident than being a skilful cyclist. There is a useful UK government website for parents and teachers which describes a fictitious town called Welltown. It teaches children aged between five and seven years old about personal, social and health issues. In particular, there are learning activities which your child can access about cars, road crossing and personal safety when outside the home. The web address can be found in the Resources section of this chapter.

Getting on your bike
Tips and hints

These are a number of tips and hints to help get your child started:

- The traditional way to teach cycling, by running along holding the child up, is still the fastest and best if an undersized bike is not available. It is important that you don't hold the handlebars (your child can't learn the feel of balancing if you are taking control of the bike). If you hold on to the saddle or any other part of the bike, your child will not necessarily realize if they are leaning a bit to one side or the other, because you will be correcting for them. You should not make any attempt to steer your child; just let the bike go where it will.

- This is not much fun for you, especially if you are tall and have to lean over to hold your child. This can lead to you suffering from a back injury as you bend and twist to control a heavy weight. The combination of bending, twisting and supporting a weight is high risk and should be avoided at all costs.

- An alternative way to support your child is to use a manual handling belt. These belts were originally designed for use in hospitals for moving patients who only needed a little extra support when moving between bed and chair or very short walks. However, for supporting your child as they learn to cycle, they fit nicely around the child's body whilst allowing you to give them some security if they wobble too far over by use of the handle on the back. Information on this product can be found in the Resources section.

Activities

Before balance is achieved, your child will need to practise the skills of steering the bike and breaking. Each of these activities builds on to the one before until your child is ready to get going on their bike.

Riding a bike is a form of exercise and, just like doing a warm-up before you run on a soccer pitch or start exercises in a gym, you should consider warming up before getting on the bike. This not only gets the muscles warmed up and ready for action but can help the balance system prepare for bike riding. This doesn't need to be fancy or exhausting! A few good stretches of the body from top to toe followed by some gentle jogging is a good start. Running and making sudden changes of direction on your command or dodging around obstacles is good. Hopping and skipping games are also useful. If your child has a scooter, go for a quick ride using each leg in turn for balance and the other for scooting.

Don't push me around
WHAT YOU NEED
Bike; things to act as 'markers'

WHAT YOU DO
Walk with bike in straight lines then turning lefts and rights, straight, turning corners, triangles, squares and circles, in and out of 'markers' (this can be anything that you have to hand as long as it's visible enough to weave in and out of).

Stop
WHAT YOU NEED
Bike

WHAT YOU DO
Pushing bike around, stop on verbal command by pulling on both brakes. Now practise getting on and getting off the bike safely, keeping hold of the brakes to keep the bike still.

Scoot
WHAT YOU NEED
Bike

WHAT YOU DO
With the pedals off the bike, practise moving in straight lines first then circles to the right and then left. You can also use cones or tin cans to learn more precise steering. Try to stop and start on command. It is important to learn the following command right from the beginning 'Feet down... Brakes on!'

The 'ready stance'

WHAT YOU NEED
Bike

WHAT YOU DO
Sitting astride the bike, take the weight through the left foot and hold the handlebars with the brakes on. Use the right foot to press the pedal backwards and round until it reaches the highest position. Rest the right foot on top of the pedal. This is the 'ready stance'. If it is easier for your child he can use the left foot. Practise this several times and include it in your routine when working on bike skills.

Push off

WHAT YOU NEED
Bike; pavement chalks or things to act as markers (cones)

WHAT YOU DO
After practising the 'ready stance', now release the brakes and practise pushing the right pedal forwards, round and down in one smooth, continuous movement. Once enough speed is gained, both feet can be placed on to the pedals and continuous cycling can begin. Speed is important here, as without it, it makes balancing on the bike much more difficult.

Off we go! – This won't happen overnight but eventually your child will reach the stage where they need less support from you (perhaps just a light hand on their back for confidence). You can make some simple courses with straight lines and gentle curves (use pavement chalks to do this or markers) to allow your child to get a better sense of balancing and steering. When your child can do this well, introduce gentle slopes and bumpy ground.

Enrol in a cycling skills course

In the UK many schools run cycling proficiency courses for children in Year Six as part of their Physical Education curriculum. However, if this is not the case, many cities have Road Safety Centres that run courses in the school holidays.

Some children's muscles may never be strong enough for them to ride a bike for a reasonable length of time or on hilly areas. There are companies who sell bikes which have an assistive motor which 'kicks in' when the cyclist needs a little extra help. Your child will need to be at least 14 years old to use one of these. See the Resources section.

R **Resources**

Online road safety activities

Welltown: www.welltown.gov.uk
  Road, car and personal safety website with interactive games for children aged 5–7 years.

Bicycles

Bikes 2U Direct (Highfield Cycles): www.bikes2udirect.com (tag-a-long bikes) (UK)

Electric Bikes Direct/The Cycle Station: www.electricbikesdirect.co.uk
  10 Station Parade, South Street, Lancing BN15 8AA;
  Telephone: +44 (0) 1903 753632; Email: info@electricbikesdirect.co.uk

Kudu Bikes: www.kudubikes.co.uk
  1 Raynes Court, Charcoals Way, Upper Wensleydale Business Park,
  Hawes, N Yorks DL8 3UW; Telephone: +44 (0) 1969 666088;
  Email: info@kudubikes.co.uk
  For tag-a-long bikes.

LikeaBike Jumper: child's trainer bike

Mission Cycles: www.missioncycles.co.uk
  Unit 3, The Alders, Seven Mile Lane, Mereworth, Kent ME18 5JG;
  Telephone: +44 (0) 1622 815678
  For large trikes and electric bikes.

PowaCycle: www.powacycle.co.uk
  Akhter House, Perry Road, Harlow, Essex CM18 7PN;
  Telephone: +44 (0) 1279 821243; Email: info@powacycle.co.uk

Quest 88: www.childrenstricycles.com (UK)
  Aston Street, Shifnal, Shropshire TF11 8DW;
  Telephone: +44 (0) 1952 463050; Email: info@childrenstricycles.com

Rotary Australia: www.rotarybike.com
  Power-assisted bicycles.

Urban Mover UM36: electric mountain bike

Veloteq: www.veloteq.com (US)

Accessories

Ashe Equestrian, the Equestrian Store: www.theequestrianstore.com
For neoprene half chaps (UK)

Benefitsnow: www.benefitsnowshop.co.uk
Comfy kids handling belt

Bike trails

See your local press or contact your local council for information on safe
places to ride your bike and great bike trails.

Safety

Royal Society for the Prevention of Accidents: www.rospa.co.uk/roadsafety

World Health Organization (2007) Youth and Road Safety. Switzerland: WHO.
Accessed on 07/11/07 at http://whqlibdoc.who.int/publications/2007/
9241595116_eng.pdf

References

Bike For All: www.bikeforall.net

Gallahue, D. and Ozmun, J. (2002) Understanding Motor Development –
Infants, Children, Adolescents and Adults, 5th ed. New York: McGraw Hill.

League of American Bicyclists: bikeleague@bikeleague.org
1612 K Street NW, Suite 800, Washington, DC 2000, USA 6;
Telephone: +1 (202) 822 1333

Sheridan, M.D. (1975) Children's Developmental Progress. Windsor, CT:
NFER Publishing Company.

Why Cycle: www.whycycle.co.uk/children-tagalong.htm
Provides information on tag-a-long or trailer bikes.

5 THROWING, CATCHING AND BAT AND BALL GAMES

Ball games, whether organized or recreational, are a great social activity and don't have to be played at a competitive level. You can play by yourself, with a friend or as part of a group. Whether it's 'Keepie Uppie' with a balloon, 'Splash and Dash' with a beach ball in the swimming pool on your holidays or even juggling, indoors or out, they all help to develop a variety of skills:

- eye/hand co-ordination
- eye/foot co-ordination
- manipulation
- visual tracking
- co-ordination of the whole body
- control and force of movement
- rhythm and timing
- agility
- anticipation
- attention
- speed of reactions
- balance whilst moving
- sense of direction
- working with others and communication.

(?)   *Where does it go wrong?...those frustrating times*

As children progress through school there is an increasing demand in Physical Education lessons to develop ball skills for small team games. Once they move up to secondary school, the demands increase and there is an expectation that children will have a reasonable mastery over these skills and can put them into practice in larger team sports. Most of the children we have met report to us that they find ball games very difficult. See Table 5.1 for a list of common areas of difficulty.

Improving throwing, catching and striking

In order to be able to throw, catch and strike (hit or kick) a ball, your child needs a sense of rhythm and timing, speed, force and flow of movement. These concepts can be practised in a variety of situations and will therefore be more easily transferred to other physical activities.

Rhythm

We all have an inbuilt sense of rhythm. Some of us more than others! Think about the rhythm of breathing, your heart beating or your pulse. We move with rhythm because it is more energy efficient than stopping and starting, and your brain responds to patterns and rhythms. We use rhythm every day in walking, running and climbing stairs. We also use it in the pattern of our day into night which helps us with our sense of organization and sense of time. These things happen without much thought or effort involved. In ball skills, a sense of rhythm is essential for the smooth, co-ordinated actions required for accuracy. Next time there is sport on television, sit down with your child and watch how a soccer player runs up to and kicks a ball or how a tennis player tosses up a ball before swinging the racquet up and over to serve it. Think about the movements as though they are part of a dance.

You can help your child move with rhythm by practising clapping to a count and also clapping or even counting to a piece of music which has a strong beat (1, 2 – 1, 2 – 1, 2 or 1, 2, 3, 4 – 1, 2, 3, 4). If your child is sitting down with eyes closed he will be able to concentrate more easily on this. Another trick is to use the bed like a giant drum where your child lies in the centre as you bounce the bed with your hands.

Table 5.1 Areas of difficulty in ball games

Difficulty	Possible reason
Difficulty throwing the ball forwards, often shooting it up into the air.	Swinging the arm through too quickly or letting go too late. Rooting the feet firmly and holding the body stiffly can prevent the throwing arm moving smoothly with rhythm to release the ball with precision. This is often due to poor stability in the body.
Difficulty gauging how hard or how softly to throw the ball.	Grasping the ball too tightly and therefore not being able to release it on time.
	Not being able to visually judge the distance the ball is required to travel.
	Not having a good sensory awareness from the muscles and joints which tell the brain about where and how we are moving.
Eyes and hands for catching or eyes and feet for kicking not working together to meet the oncoming ball.	Inability to track the oncoming ball thereby not 'seeing it' in time to get hands or feet ready.
	Not having good standing balance can make it difficult to move the feet and adjust the body position to catch or trap an oncoming ball when it is thrown slightly out of reach.
	Clasping the hands too quickly causing the ball to bounce off the hands or too slowly, missing it completely or causing the ball to bounce off the body.
	The child has not yet developed whole body co-ordination.
Inability to follow the moving ball with the eyes as it travels towards them.	This may be due to a visual field (focusing) difficulty for example, not being able to see the ball coming out from the 'background' until it is almost in front of them.
Turning away from the oncoming ball or closing the eyes for fear of being hit by it.	Same reasons as above but also a developmental stage of catching that all children go through before learning to trap the ball against their body.
When they do grasp or catch the ball, they do not move to 'absorb' the catch and then have difficulty repositioning the body to return the throw.	Holding the body rigidly with feet planted firmly facing forwards can mean that the child does not have good balance or stability in the body to make the necessary adjustments to change body position with speed and accuracy.
Difficulty with balance either when the child is standing still or on the move and having to respond to an unpredictable moving object.	Poor body stability from weak posture muscles or instability around the shoulder joints.

This means that he can 'feel' the beat through his whole body. Bouncing and counting simultaneously can also help to instil this sense of rhythm as will marching on the spot or around the room swinging your arms to music. The arms should move in opposite directions to the legs. For example: right leg and foot swing forwards and the left arm swings forwards at the same time. (The right arm swings back at the same time and the left leg is pushing backwards on the ground.)

Speed

When considering the speed of movement it will help your child to appreciate the different sensations of speed if you can use words to describe the movements before and during the action. To describe *fast* movement for example you could use words like: *quick, sudden, speedy, flat out, like a flash* and *like a shot*. You can also describe that their muscles should feel tight. Use your tone of voice and the speed you say the words to emphasise speed too.

To describe *slow* movement you can use words such as: *snail-like, tortoise-like, leisurely, unhurried, carefully* and *like slow motion*. The muscles should feel relaxed.

Practise the throwing action (underarm or overarm) without a ball at first to learn the concepts of *fast* and *slow*. You can increase the sensory awareness of speed in the movement by wearing wrist weights or, if out of doors, throw a heavy object like a weighted ball or tin of beans into a *big* space. Ask your child to put the different sensations into words and describe what they are feeling.

Force

Force is a really important concept to learn as this will help your child gauge how hard to throw, strike or even kick an object in order to reach a target. Without this, they cannot judge the results of an ineffective throw, strike or kick and change their practice to make it more successful the next time. 'Force' also relates to how much speed and strength is required in a run up for example, just before hitting a ball with a bat in racquet sports or kicking a ball. The two extremes of force are *strong* and *light*. Words you can use to help with the concept of strong are: *strong, powerful, heavy, explosive*. The muscles will feel heavy or tense. To describe a *light* force you can use words like *easy, weak, fluffy, wispy* and *feathery*. When moving with light force, the muscles will feel loose.

Flow

Flow relates to how smooth or jerky a movement is and can be difficult to sense and control if your muscles are slightly floppy or your balance is poor. This can make controlling the arms and legs less precise. In therapy terms we call this 'grading' of movement. Flow of movement can either be *controlled* or *free flowing* (relaxed). *Controlled* movement can be described in words like: *robotic, jerky, stiff, rigid, firm* and the muscles feel tight. *Free flowing* movement can be described in words such as: *smooth, fluid, continuous, graceful, light on your feet, supple*. Muscles move easily.

Notes for grown-ups

You can play some ball games indoors but if you do, use soft, woolly pom-pom balls, balloons, bubbles or even shower puffs so that you don't damage any of the family heirlooms. Make sure there is sufficient space. It is also helpful to keep pets out of the way to prevent trips and falls.

Playing the games either sitting or lying not only helps with the physical demands of the task; it also helps to keep the 'ball' down nearer to the floor level.

Tips and hints

CATCH AND THROW

- The larger the object being thrown, the easier it is to catch. Textured balls with a softer surface may also be easier to grasp, such as 'Koosh balls' or bean bags (see Resources).

- As mentioned earlier, catching requires the child to be able to look and follow a moving object whilst being able to get their hands in the right place to catch the object. If your child turns his head away from an oncoming object being thrown for fear of being hit, try reducing the distance between the thrower and the catcher. Bouncing the ball to your child will also slow down the speed and give him time to respond to the oncoming ball. Try using a balloon or a knotted chiffon scarf as these move more slowly. If your child does not like balloons, you can purchase some balloon covers. See the Resources section for suppliers.

- Practise catching and throwing in different positions, for example, lying on his front, sitting with legs astride (open) or kneeling up tall. This takes away the need for your child to concentrate on his balance at the same time as co-ordinating his eyes and hands.

CATCHING

- To practise catching, you can give your child a lightweight mesh basket to hold in which to catch the oncoming objects. This relies quite heavily on the accuracy of the person throwing but enables your child to be more successful to begin with. Alternatively, you could buy some fabric catching gloves which have a raised loopy pile on to which balls with added strips of Velcro will fasten very easily. This takes away the need for your child to close their hands around the ball (look for 'Stickymitts' or 'No Miss Catch Mitts and Velcro Balls': see Resources section, and you can also buy them in many shops).

- Select catching equipment that is matched to the size, confidence and skill level of your child so that he will be motivated to participate more actively. Don't necessarily think that catching and throwing always has to be with balls. Try some of the following:
  - scarves (knotted chiffon or shower puffs)

- balloons (try filling these with water – this is a great game for the summer)
- balls of wool. Do you remember making woolly pom pom balls? These are great as they don't roll too far. This is also good for developing manipulation and planning skills, so get your child to make his own (see Appendix 2)!
- beach balls are large and soft to catch if you don't over inflate them
- paper balls made of crushed paper bound with masking tape or commercially bought Chinese-style 'Plusballs' which you inflate with a straw (see Resource section)
- rubbish bags or grocery bags filled with a balloon or newspaper
- welly boots – have a 'welly wanging' competition!
- rolled-up pair of old socks
- tennis ball tied into a stocking leg – this creates a 'tail'
- horseshoes (plastic)
- frisbees (plastic or cloth)
- small soft toys.

- When passing or throwing the 'ball' always ask your child if he is ready. This alerts him to the presence of the ball and keeps him on task. It might help if your child can stand on a marker like a carpet tile or in a hoop to focus him on where to stand. Once your child can catch the bigger, slower moving objects successfully without the use of the basket or catching gloves, he needs to practise catching objects in his hands rather than trapping them against his body. He also needs to practise making subtle adjustments to his body posture. This means taking steps away from his standing position to catch a ball outside his reach, that is, leaning back or stepping back if necessary to 'absorb' the oncoming ball, forwards if the ball is thrown too short or sideways if the throw is going wide.

- The next step is for you to change your starting position before each throw so your child has to adjust his standing position to follow the ball. You can make this faster and less predictable to make the task harder for your child. Another increase in difficulty is for you to stand still and your child to move as you throw the ball. This means he has to be aware of his body position, the direction of the oncoming ball, his balance and getting his eyes and hands working together to catch it. Once your child can catch on the move, he's ready to catch and return the ball to you or to throw against a wall.

THROWING

- To begin to learn to throw, you could start your child off with smaller objects aiming to throw 'underarm' to land in a wide box, bin, hoop or target which is placed quite near to him. This can then be made more difficult by having the child throw an object at a smaller target, or at a target that's further away, or one that's moving.

- If throwing the ball is really difficult for your child, to begin with he could try rolling a ball down a half (open) piece of plastic guttering or cardboard tube so that he can practise releasing the ball and aiming the tube at the intended target.

- The skill of rolling the ball is actually quite a useful one as it requires a slow rhythmical arm swing followed by releasing the ball when the child is focused on the target. It teaches all the skills we discussed earlier in the chapter, that is, rhythm, speed, force and flow, and leads to learning not only the underarm throwing action but also bowling for games such as ten pin bowling, skittles and crown green bowling, cricket, rounders and baseball and the toss up for the tennis serve.

- Practise different styles of throwing, for example: underarm, overarm with either or both hands and with both hands pushing the ball away from the chest.

- In order to encourage accuracy when throwing, your child can practise by throwing against a wall. Place a small marker or sticker about eye level and get your child to point at the target (this helps to reinforce the eye-hand movement required to hit a target). When throwing the ball, encourage your child to keep looking at the marker because this helps him to focus his attention on the target and prevents him from throwing the ball accidentally up into the air.

- Develop your child's awareness of his hands before catching and throwing games by rubbing them together several times and then clapping. The tingling feeling helps to 'wake up the hands'.

Some ideas to start with

Bubbles

You can either buy cheap bubble mix or make your own from concentrated washing-up liquid and a little water. We have included some bubble recipes in Appendix 3.

- Blow the bubbles and watch them fall and stamp on them.
- Let them fall and pop them with the index finger.
- Let them fall and 'clap' with both hands to pop them.
- Catch one in each hand at the same time.
- Catch by numbers – catch one bubble at a time, then quickly call out 'two', then 'three,' etc. Change the game by calling out numbers randomly. Alternatively, throw a dice and catch the number of bubbles to match the 'dots'. This will help to improve reaction time, speed and accuracy as well as working at different levels, visually tracking the bubbles as they fall.

Balloons

- Drop a balloon, let it bounce, and then catch it.
- Throw the balloon into the air and catch it.
- See how high you can throw the balloon and still catch it.
- Throw the balloon into the air and see how many times you can clap your hands before you catch it.
- Throw the balloon against the wall and catch it.
- Throw the balloon back and forth with a friend. Pat it back with the hand which acts as a 'bat'.
- If your child is nervous of balloons, try using a balloon cover (see Resources section).
- You can pour some dried rice or lentils into a balloon, then inflate it to make it slightly heavier and noisy. This can make it easier to follow and catch.

Launch boards

A launch board propels the ball into the air directly in front of you and you don't then need to be skilled at tossing the ball into the air. Try games like 'Kick-a-Flick', which are commercially available (check out the Resources section).

Place a rolled-up pair of socks on the launch end of the board (the low end of the board). Encourage your child to stand at the other end with hands ready to catch. Stomp down on the end of the board and the sock ball should fly up into the air in front of you. Don't worry if your child cannot catch straight away. It is important for him to learn to watch and anticipate where the 'ball is going'. Play games to see how high he can make the sock ball go. Try different objects and see which ones 'fly' better than others. Play games where your child 'stomps' on the launch pad and then tries to catch.

Toys

There are a number of great commercially available toys which help with ball skills. One of our favourites we call the 'whizzer'; it is also known as a 'speedball'. A rugby ball-shaped object has two lengths of cord running through the centre of it. Both ends of the cords have a handle attached to them and the game is played by two people. Starting with hands held together one person opens their arms, which shoots the ball towards the other person. As the ball approaches the second person, they open their hands and send it back. The ball shuttles between the pair. This game also helps with upper arm strength and can be played indoors and out (see Resources section).

Look out for different bats in the toy shops such as 'boom bats' or large-headed bats and giant shuttlecocks.

Games to play

How far?

WHAT YOU NEED
A variety of things to throw, for example, sponge, balls of wool, shower puffs

WHAT YOU DO
Play this outside. Encourage your child to throw the various objects predicting which ones they think will travel the furthest/least and why. This will also help with language skills and is a good science experiment. What happens if the objects are wet or if it is windy?

Directional ball

WHAT YOU NEED
Small ball

WHAT YOU DO
Standing, with legs hip width apart, your child should use the hands to move the ball around the body.

- Figure eights – push ball around ankles and feet making a figure of eight (8) shape.

- Pass the ball hand to hand around the waist.
- Pass the ball hand to hand around the head.
- Pass ball front to back and vice versa through legs.
- Pass ball under the thigh, lifting foot off the floor each time (like standing on one leg).
- Lying on their back on the floor with knees bent and feet flat on the floor, your child needs to pass the ball from one hand to the other by lifting his bottom off the floor (like making a bridge). Staying in this position, pass the ball under each leg by lifting them up one at a time off the floor.

Hot rocks
WHAT YOU NEED
Large soccer size ball

WHAT YOU DO
Play in pairs or with a few others. Pass the ball (hot rock) by throwing it to another person as quickly as you can (don't get your fingers burnt!). Practise different kinds of two-handed, one-handed, overhead, side and chest-level passes.

Trash mash
WHAT YOU NEED
Scrunched up newspaper balls and a large low box/washing basket

WHAT YOU DO
After scrunching up the paper (which is also good for fine motor skills), throw the paper balls into the basket. Start by standing fairly close to the target. Once they have mastered this increase the challenge by having them step progressively further away from it. Change the game by playing in a different position, for example, lying on tummies or kneeling up tall.

Snowball fight
WHAT YOU NEED
Scrunched up newspaper balls

WHAT YOU DO
This is best played with a few players. Everyone has some 'snowballs'. Mark out a line with players standing each side of the line. On the command 'go' everyone launches their snowballs. See who can get the most snowballs to the other side.

Light up the sky
WHAT YOU NEED
A torch and a fly swatter; a slightly darkened room

WHAT YOU DO
Switch the torch on and off, shining it either on the wall or floor. As the light comes on, your child has to 'swat' the light before you switch it off. Work within a small space around the child to begin with and leave the light on to allow them time to adjust their reactions. As they develop their speed, change the levels you are working on, for example, from floor to wall and back again (not too high of course) as well as speeding up the time you switch on/off the light.

Hoopster
WHAT YOU NEED
A hula hoop and some space (grass or paved area)

WHAT YOU DO
Stand the hoop up on its end. Encourage your child to roll the hoop in a straight line towards a goal, for example, a chair. Now see how far the hoop can be rolled with one push. Try rolling two hoops at the same time.

Skittles
WHAT YOU NEED
Large ball; empty pop bottles or commercial skittles

WHAT YOU DO
This is a good old-fashioned favourite game. Roll the ball and knock over the skittles. To develop the game, use different objects to knock over as well as different balls to roll or throw.

Progression ball
WHAT YOU NEED
Play in pairs; ball

WHAT YOU DO
In pairs, stand about the same distance from a marked point, for example an empty ice cream container or upturned wastepaper basket. Throw a ball (or bean bag) to a partner. If it is caught, the partner takes a step backwards, but if the ball (or bean bag) is dropped, both partners take one step forward. If the throw does not reach the partner, the thrower takes one step forward. The winner is the one who is the greatest distance from the marker when the stop signal is given.

Outdoor bowling with paint!
WHAT YOU NEED
Ball; paint (the type used for children's art and craft); large pieces of paper or rolls of wallpaper; old play clothes

WHAT YOU DO
Have your child roll a ball in tray of paint and then roll it down a strip of paper. Yes, this is messy but great fun. Jackson Pollock eat your heart out!

Pancake toss
WHAT YOU NEED
A bean bag or a rolled-up pair of socks (pancake); lightweight bat (pretend frying pan)

WHAT YOU DO
Have a starting line and stand behind it balancing the bean bag on the bat held out in front. Begin by walking straight ahead to a finish line without tossing the 'pancake' (bean bag). To make it more fun, try to do this at a gentle jog then add in a toss or two each run! Try making it much harder still by placing obstacles to walk around... Well, we are therapists so we are allowed to be tough sometimes!

Walk and bounce

WHAT YOU NEED
Large ball

WHAT YOU DO
Encourage your child to walk and bounce the ball at the same time.
Practise just dropping it and catching it with both hands first then see
if he can 'pat' it. As he improves add a simple obstacle course for him
to navigate. Then get him to try bouncing and patting with the right
hand only, then the left only, depending on his age. You can then
decrease the size of the ball and/or add using a short-handled bat to
tap the ball.

Wall volleying and catch

WHAT YOU NEED
A large lightweight ball

WHAT YOU DO
Standing quite close to a wall, encourage your child to pat the ball
(using an underarm strike) against the wall with the palm of the hand.
Allow a bounce as this slows down the speed of the ball and allows
him to adjust his body position in time. As your child improves encourage him to take a small step backwards away from the wall. Now he
will have to adjust the force he uses. Another idea is to play the game
in pairs. You may now like to introduce a short-handled bat (see
Resources section).

Balloon volleyball

WHAT YOU NEED
Balloon; garden badminton net or piece of tape stretched across two
garden canes; other players

WHAT YOU DO
Stand either side of the net in equal numbers (like 'singles', 'doubles'
or team volleyball). Define the boundaries of the court with tape,
ribbon or a chalk line depending on the playing surface. You could
start small to begin with depending on the size of the surrounding
area, to keep the game more controlled, then increase the court size
to make the game more active. Decide who is going to serve the

balloon, then toss it into the air and hit it across the net. The opponent has to keep the balloon up in the air and hit it back across the net again to return it. You can decide how many hits you are allowed within each team (or single player if playing singles) before returning it over the net. The person to let the balloon hit the floor awards a point to the opposing team or player and a hit over the side or back lines also gives the opposition a point. This is a new Olympic and Common-wealth Games sport, so watch out for it on television. You won't be wearing the skimpy bathing suits and they won't be using balloons though!

Gone batty

WHAT YOU NEED

A large ball; a rolled-up newspaper, child's plastic golf club or upturned walking stick (something long-handled)

WHAT YOU DO

Lay out a simple obstacle course. Encourage your child to control the ball around the obstacles just using the long-handled 'bat'. To develop the game use a timer and see if your child can beat the score each time.

Catch-a-ball with a scoop

WHAT YOU NEED

A small lightweight ball (table tennis or airflow/golf practice ball); two clean, empty two-litre pop bottles or four-litre milk bottles cut diago-nally across the ends to make a wide-mouthed scoop; a partner

WHAT YOU DO

Stand opposite each other; hold your scoop by the handle. Start close together then, as you succeed in catching the ball, move further apart. Place the ball in one scoop then toss it to your partner who tries to catch it in their scoop. You could always practise on your own first to get the feel of the scoop and how to catch with it.

Flicking soccer

WHAT YOU NEED

A sheet of paper A4 or letter size; a table top

WHAT YOU DO

Begin by making your paper 'soccer ball'. Fold the paper into thirds lengthwise to make a long strip about 7 cm (3 inches) wide with the narrow edge facing you. Next, take the left-hand corner and fold it to make a triangle shape. Press it down the crease to help it stay in place. Fold the right-hand corner straight up to make another triangle and press hard along the crease. Keep folding the paper like this to make triangles all the way to the top (about six times). Fold over the top straight edge and tuck in, then use sticky tape over the top to secure it in place.

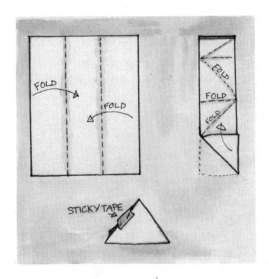

Once you have made your 'paper soccer ball' you can decorate it in your favourite team's colours on one side and your opponent's team on the other (this activity is another good one for developing fine motor skills). The 'playing field' is the table top with a small sticker or dot on the centre point and the edges of the table are the back and side lines. To play the game your opponent must stand at the opposite end of the table (on the short side). To decide who goes first, toss the ball in the air and see which side it lands on. That 'team' gets to flick first. To get started, the ball is flicked (using the index finger) down the table to the defending team. To pass the ball and stop it crossing the goal line, the players must rest their wrist and fingertips of one hand on the table (the other hand must be under the table) and push and slide the ball with their fingertips. When the ball crosses the goal line (back of the table), you score five points. Start on the centre line to play the next points. May the best player win!

R ## Resources

For a range of equipment and resources such as balloon balls, Koosh balls, Kick-a-Flick, Stickymitts and many more:

Davies Sports: www.daviessports.co.uk
  Telephone: +44 (0) 845 120 4515

Early Learning Centre: www.elc.co.uk
  Boom bats.

Growing Tree Toys: www.growingtreetoys.com (US)

KikAFlik: www.kikaflik.com (US)

Paper balls: Plusballs (see below)

Plusballs: www.plusballs.com
  Bluemead, Echo Lane, Stinchcombe, nr Dursley, Glos GL11 6BQ;
  Telephone: +44 (0) 1453 547461

School Speciality: www.schoolspecialtyonline.net (US)

Special Direct: www.specialdirect.com (UK)
  Telephone: +44 (0) 800 318 686

TTS Group: www.tts-group.co.uk

References

Beaumont, G. (1997) *Physical Education*. Southam: Scholastic.

Bissell, J., Fisher, J., Owens, C. and Polcyn, P. (1988) *Sensory Motor Handbook: A Guide For Implementing and Modifying Activities in the Classroom*. St Petersburg, FL: Sensory Integration International.

Buschner, C.A. (1994) *Teaching Children Movement Concepts and Skills: Becoming a Master Teacher*. Champaign, IL: Human Kinetics.

Macintyre, C. and McVitty, K. (2004) *Movement and Learning in Early Years: Supporting Dyspraxia (DCD) and Other Difficulties*. London: Paul Chapman Publishing.

Public Broadcasting Service: www.pbs.org/parents/fungames

Russell, J.P. (1997) *Graded Activities for Children with Motor Difficulties*. Cambridge: Cambridge University Press.

Sutherland, C. (2006) *No Gym! No Problem!* Champaign, IL: Human Kinetics.

Work Notes: www.worknotes.com/IL/Chicago/Fit4FunKidsFtiness/ap16.stm

6 SOCCER CRAZY: CAN WE KICK IT? YES WE CAN!

What can we say? Boys love their soccer, isn't that what they are all about? They will kick anything remotely round, any time, any place, anywhere, any age. They play it, watch it, talk about it and many of their role models are soccer players. So what happens if your child can't kick a ball, doesn't follow the game and finds that he might be left out of games at school or club because he can't keep up?

At the end of the day, everyone is an individual and many will not be interested in sporty activities. What you will need to find out is whether your child is not interested in soccer because he prefers science or the arts, for example, or whether he just lacks the skills and self-confidence. If he loves soccer but doesn't have the skills to participate as a player, then you could develop his interest in coaching or officiating instead. This means that, socially, he will be able to keep up with the playground discussions on soccer and not have to feel left out. As therapists we may not have a working knowledge of the 'offside rule' but we do know what skills you need to kick a ball around!

Soccer can develop many skills:

- balance and co-ordination
- good posture
- eye/foot and eye/hand co-ordination
- body and spatial awareness
- strength and flexibility
- cardiovascular fitness
- working as part of a team

- development of social skills and sense of belonging
- learning how to co-operate and compete
- learning to express emotion and imagination through new experiences
- taking responsibility for actions
- dealing with success and failure.

Notes for grown-ups

If your child has a predisposition to certain injuries such as frequent ankle sprains or knee pains, he should be examined by the GP or a children's physiotherapist before starting any serious training.

It is important to warm up and cool down if you and your child are doing lots of running around.

Why does my child find soccer skills difficult?

There are many different aspects to why some children find soccer skills difficult, so we hope Table 6.1 helps you to pinpoint some of the reasons.

Tips and hints

Before you start it is helpful for your child to develop the mechanics of the basic movements. You will need to keep it simple. At this stage, children are more likely to be learning basic physical skills rather than soccer specific skills. The need for rhythm, timing, force and flow of movement are just as important to soccer skills as they are to throwing and catching so have a look at this section in Chapter 5.

Here are a few tips and hints before you start:

- Blow up balloons and use them to encourage your child to practise heading, kicking and dribbling.
- Use your imagination to make soccer a part of everyday tasks.
- Play with your child. You don't have to be an expert to have a casual kick around. Allow mistakes, both yours and your

child's. Have fun. Casual play is a chance to chat, laugh and bond.

- Use large light balls, like beach balls, which are slower moving and don't hurt when they hit you.

- Get the feel of the ball with hands and feet while in a sitting and kneeling position.

- Manipulate the ball with hands and feet while standing in one spot (throw in air and catch, bounce on ground, bounce once on different body parts; push ball gently with inside and outside of foot, pull it back with the sole of the foot).

- Check for understanding. Ask your child to explain what he has learned after practice or games.

- Ask children to demonstrate. Children love to be experts, especially with their parents. Also, this reinforces their understanding of soccer skills.

- Put different coloured stickers or tape on the inner side and outer side of the trainers to help your child quickly identify which part of the foot to kick with.

- Remember that success is related to the attempt not the outcome!

Kicking practice

The best way to practise this technique is against a 'keeper' (a parent or friend) who consistently serves the ball back to your child. If this is not an option, then any flat wall, ledge or flat surface can work. Begin by working on kicking still balls (meaning they must stop and trap it before kicking), then move to practising striking the ball without settling it first. There are also commercially available kicking games such as the 'Soccer Zoomer' or 'Kick Master Controller' where the balls are attached to elastic at one end and to the child or a fixed post at the other (see Resources section).

Tips and hints

- Practise the 'get ready stance'. This means standing behind the ball, feet hip width apart and eyes looking at the ball.

- At the beginning, stress keeping the head down, looking at the ball when kicking it, rather than on the target where it is to be kicked.

- Kicking a ball above the middle may result in a fall. It should be kicked between the bottom and middle.

- To make the kick strong, follow through with the kicking foot after the ball has been struck (in the direction of the goal or target).

- Begin by walking and then jogging with the ball, keeping it close to the feet, using the inside of the feet and keeping the ball on the ground.

- Play 'Which can you kick the furthest, a woollen ball or a rubber ball?'

- Can you hold a ball with both hands and kick it out of your hands?

- Kick a ball seven times (or whatever your number focus is for the day, week or month).

- Tether a ball to a sturdy frame using elastic (also check out Kick Master Footballs or similar – see Resources section).

- Take off your shoes and socks. Sit on the floor with both feet flat and knees bent in between your arms. Try kicking the ball out of your hands. Then try to do it with a bounce between each kick.

- Place a bean bag or rolled-up sock on your child's foot and ask him to try and kick it off.

- Work on balance. Begin games by incorporating balance activities, such as standing on one foot, which eventually leads to striking the ball.

- Stand in the 'get ready stance' and place one foot on top of the soccer ball. Try moving the ball backwards, forwards and round in a small circle. Try with the other foot too. How many seconds can you keep the ball moving for?

Some children find complex rules and the requirements of proper team positions and play difficult to follow. Game rules and strategies should therefore be kept simple, involving only the most basic skills, and include no more than two to five children per team.

Table 6.1 Areas of difficulty in soccer skills

Difficulty	Possible reason
Difficulty projecting the ball forwards, often shooting it up into the air.	Kicking the leg through too quickly and not aiming at the goal. Not having sufficient balance to control the leg in order to move smoothly with rhythm and precision. This is often due to poor body stability. Using the wrong part of the foot to kick with, for example, hooking underneath the ball with the front of the foot or toes.
Difficulty gauging how hard or how softly to kick the ball.	Not being able to visually judge the distance the ball is required to travel.
	Not receiving good sensory information from the muscles and joints which tells the brain about where and how we are moving.
Eyes and feet not working together to meet the oncoming ball.	Inability to track the oncoming ball thereby not 'seeing it' in time to get posture and feet ready.
	Not having very good balance can make it difficult to move the feet and adjust the body position to catch or trap an oncoming ball when it is passed slightly out of reach.
	The child has not yet developed whole body co-ordination yet.
Inability to follow the moving ball with the eyes as it travels towards him.	This may be due to a visual field (focusing) difficulty for example, not being able to see the ball coming out from the 'background' until it is almost in front of him.
Turning away from the oncoming ball or closing the eyes for fear of being hit by it.	Same reasons as above or fear of being hit by a heavy ball.
Difficulty with balance whilst the child standing still or on the move and having to respond to an often unpredictable moving object.	Weaker ability in the muscles that help to stabilize the body and the leg joints that are needed for balancing (this is sometimes referred to as weak postural stability or instability around the limb girdles).

Games to play

We have had a look at the skills needed to kick a soccer ball and given some ideas of how to practise these at home. There are also some excellent websites, which give many more coaching tips and activities, listed at the end of the chapter.

Ball stretching
WHAT YOU NEED
Large ball

WHAT YOU DO
Here are lots of little games in one:

- Stand with legs apart and roll the ball with hands in a figure of eight in and out of the legs.
- Place one foot in front of the other and roll the ball around the front foot ten times, then switch.
- Sit down with legs extended in front, and roll the ball towards and around the feet and return along the other side of the leg.
- Sit with legs open in a 'V' shape and move the ball in an outline around the body, including the back. This activity makes the children stretch without realizing it. They also warm up the muscles.

I can do this, can you?
WHAT YOU NEED
Large ball

WHAT YOU DO
Lead this game first, saying, 'I can do this (dribble with your left foot, kick as far as you can, etc.) can you?' and then your child has to mimic you. Now ask your child to come and lead the activity.

Ball retrieving
WHAT YOU NEED
Several balls (large and small)

WHAT YOU DO
Start by throwing a few balls and scatter them around the playing area. On the word 'go' your child must retrieve the balls as quickly as possible and bring them back any way he wants to (carry in one hand, both hands, hold on top of head, etc.). Let him come up with his own ideas.

Off to the zoo
WHAT YOU NEED
Large ball

WHAT YOU DO
This game starts without a ball. Have your child stand in the playing space, then call out an animal. Your child then walks around mimicking that animal. After a few goes at this add the ball. Now he must dribble while being an animal.

Shadow dribbling
WHAT YOU NEED
Play in pairs; large balls for each child

WHAT YOU DO
Have children work in pairs, each player with a ball. The leader dribbles the ball while the second player follows, also dribbling. Encourage creative dribbling, for example, changes in direction, pace and technique. On the word 'change' the 'players' turn so that the player that was behind is now in the front.

Dribble around
WHAT YOU NEED
Play in pairs; large ball

WHAT YOU DO
Face your partner with ten paces between you. The player with the ball stands in the 'ready stance' then moves forwards, dribbling the ball by tapping it gently from foot to foot (the ball should never be more than a few centimetres (inches) away from the feet to make sure that it is under control). Dribble the ball with control around your partner, either to the left or right, and return to the starting position. Once

back, stop the ball with the foot, turn your foot outwards and kick the ball to your partner. Your partner should stop and trap the ball before dribbling it around you.

Ouch!
WHAT YOU NEED
Large ball; more than one player

WHAT YOU DO
The children will be working with a ball in a small, confined space. One 'player' must dribble the ball around the space until it can be kicked towards the other 'player' who is running around within the same space. The aim is to avoid being hit by a ball. Every time the other player is struck by the ball he yells 'Ouch', louder based on the strength of the hit and of course a degree of amateur dramatics! This game teaches ball control and shooting as well as making the children think about strategies and space.

Traffic lights
WHAT YOU NEED
Large ball

WHAT YOU DO
Stand with your back to your child who dribbles the ball to you. You call out 'green', 'amber' and 'red' and turn around. At this point your child has to stop the ball with his foot and then shoot the ball to you.

Traffic cop
WHAT YOU NEED
Large ball

WHAT YOU DO
Dribble ball around the playing space. The adult gives different commands and the child has to move in different ways with the ball:

- motorway/freeway – run or jog
- country lane – walk
- police car – walk very slowly with the ball then stop the ball with the foot!

Treasure hunt

WHAT YOU NEED

Large ball; treasures – these can be any interesting items – link them to a game of 'pirates' or even make letter cards to spell to bring back and work out the 'magic answer' related to soccer

WHAT YOU DO

Dribble ball to find the 'treasures' which are scattered on the ground. As your child gets to a treasure, he collects it to bring back to the den.

Draw

WHAT YOU NEED

Large ball

WHAT YOU DO

Standing with the ball in front of him, your child places his foot on top of the ball and tries to draw shapes with the ball using the sole of the foot. Just try simple shapes such as a line up/down, from right to left/left to right and a circle.

Paperbag kickball

WHAT YOU NEED

Medium-size paper bag; newspaper; stapler; masking tape

WHAT YOU DO

Tear newspaper up into strips or pieces. Stuff newspaper into paper bag until it is about three quarters full, compacting so it forms a 'roundish' shape. Fold the top down and staple it. Cover the staples with a piece of tape to secure the bag. You may wish to paint the ball a bright or fluorescent colour.

Skittle ball

WHAT YOU NEED

Five 'skittles' (milk cartons, pop bottles, tins, shoe boxes); medium-sized ball

WHAT YOU DO

Place skittles about 10 cm (4 inches) apart in a 'V' formation. Stand about 2 metres (6 feet 6 inches) from the skittles and kick the ball to knock them down. To make it more difficult, you can increase the distance between the skittles and the kicker. If you fill the pop bottles with water or sand to make them heavier, they become harder to knock down.

High kneel soccer

WHAT YOU NEED
Slightly deflated beach ball; a carpeted area, but where there is plenty of room; more than one player

WHAT YOU DO
Rather than playing in a standing position, get down onto your knees and then kneel up 'tall'. You now walk and kick with your knees rather than your feet. Try some tackles (no hands!) and see if you can score some goals. Make sure you are all wearing thick trousers so you don't get sore knees.

Marbles

WHAT YOU NEED
Play in pairs; a large ball for each child; a starting line

WHAT YOU DO
Standing with his back to the starting line, the first 'player' throws his ball over his head. The second 'player' then kicks his ball from the starting point and tries to hit the ball that was thrown. Play alternates by kicks until one ball is hit. The players then change over and start again.

Crab soccer

WHAT YOU NEED
Slightly deflated beach ball; a carpeted area, but where there is plenty of room; more than one player

WHAT YOU DO
Rather than playing in a standing position, sit down on the floor with your hands behind you and push up so that your bottom is in the air (like a crab). Use this position to move to get the ball. Kick the ball using your feet to score a goal. Maintaining this position for some children is very hard. Let them 'bottom shuffle' if this is the case.

Resources

Coaching and guidance

BBC: www.bbc.co.uk/science/hottopics/football

Footy4kids: www.footy4kids.co.uk

Give Me Football: www.givemefootball.com/coaching (UK)

Kids First Soccer: www.kidsfirstsoccer.com (US)
    Ideas for practice.

Special Olympics: www.specialolympics.org (regional options)
    Useful for coaching guides and games to play.

Virtual Library of Sport: www.sportsvl.com/overview.htm

Equipment

Davies Sports: www.daviessports.co.uk
    Telephone: +44 (0) 845 120 4515

Early Learning Centre: www.elc.co.uk
    Soccer Zoomer

Kickmaster Close Control Trainer (MV Sports & Leisure):
    www.mailorderexpress.com/MV

References

Junior Soccer Coach: www.juniorsoccercoach.com

Pike, E. (2001) *Ready to go! Ideas for PE Games KS2*. Southam: Scholastic.

www.calstatela.edu/faculty/dfrankl/lsnplns1.htm

www.ehow.com/how_5085_know-skills-are
    How to know what skills are important for a beginning soccer player.

7 RUGBY: A GAME OF UP AND UNDER

We just couldn't write a book on physical activities that didn't include something about the Welsh national game! Children in Wales start to learn rugby skills in primary school and this is probably the same for most children in the UK. The PE lessons from Year Three to Six teach 'invasion games' which gives the grounding for many different types of team ball games. This might be rugby, soccer, hockey, basketball, netball or even tennis. Children learn to find spaces on the playing field in order to receive and keep the ball. They also learn about strategies and tactics to outwit opponents, how to get into the opponent's territory and good positions for scoring goals. Whilst developing these skills, the children will also be learning basic ball handling skills, running, dodging and swerving skills. Once in secondary school, these elementary skills are developed to learn more specialized ball handling techniques and full game situations, so not much time is spent on basic throwing and catching activities.

We have already considered the basic skills your child will need for throwing and catching in Chapter 5 and looked at kicking the ball in Chapter 6, but for rugby, the handling skills are quite different.

To see why your child might have problems in these areas refer back to these two chapters. However, in rugby the ball is passed sideways and slightly behind you as you run forwards, which is quite a skilled manoeuvre. Your child will need to be able to work across his body, which in co-ordination terms can be difficult. Take time to practise the skills and get used to the feel and flight of this rather odd-shaped ball at home before needing to do it at school.

Notes for grown-ups

In order to maintain your child's self-esteem you might approach skills practice as being an essential part of any sports training. Even professional players practise the basics at *every* training session. (It doesn't always look like it but it's true!)

Passing and receiving the ball

To pass and receive the ball you need to learn the 'lateral pass'. When catching the ball, keep the hands at chest height and the arms stretched out sideways. The hands are the target for the thrower. The hips and legs face forwards in the direction you would be moving (if you were doing this on the run). The head, shoulders and upper body are turned to look at the player sending the ball and the ball itself. The thrower and catcher should be close together to begin with.

Practising the lateral pass

It would be ideal to have three people, and you need a rugby ball (the size depends on the size of the child practising).

- Stand in a staggered line facing forwards.

- Player number 1 stands slightly forwards of the child and player number 3 stands slightly behind him.

- Player number 1 passes the ball to the child in the centre. Your child should turn their upper body towards number 1, arms out sideways and hands at chest height ready to catch the oncoming ball. With a smooth flowing action, your child should swing his arms across his body (keeping the feet and lower body facing forwards) out sideways to pass the ball to the waiting hands of player number 3. Remember that the hands of the waiting player are the target for the pass, so remind your child to look where he is going to throw the ball before letting go, then follow through with the hands.

- Player number 3 should take a few steps forwards, followed by your child until they are both standing ahead of player number 1.

- Pass the ball back down the line to reach player number 1.
- Repeat until you reach the end of the garden or a preset course. Once you can do this standing still to the left and right, introduce a walking pace, then a gentle jog.

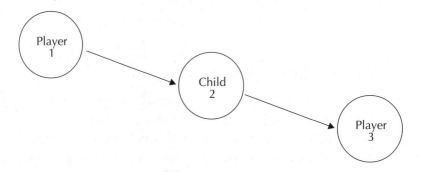

Catching a high ball

Rugby is a game of throwing and kicking and when the ball is not being passed sideways, it is being thrown high in the 'line out' or being caught from a high kick. To catch a high ball, your child must learn to get underneath the ball and keep their eyes on it at all times. For this, they need to be aware of their feet in relation to their body and be conscious of any obstacles, e.g. others around them. Using a brightly coloured ball might help identify it from the background colour of the sky. The hands must be above the head with the elbows close together, because rather than catching the ball, the hands are used to guide the ball into a 'cradle' that is formed between the hands, forearms and body. This is rather like the way a young child will catch and gather a ball into their body rather than catch it in their hands.

Your child should be encouraged to make his hands as big as possible by spreading his fingers. Finally one arm and shoulder and one hip and leg on the same side of the body should be leading forwards as though ready to run with the ball as soon as it is safely caught.

Quick hands

Quick hands are about passing the ball before you catch it! Think of the ball as being a hot potato that you don't want to wrap your hands around but need to guide to the next person. Have a look at the Chapter 5 for some games that might be adapted to practise this skill.

Kicking

The kicking aspect of rugby is about getting the ball down the pitch towards the try line or to kick to try and score a goal over the posts. There is no dribbling as such.

In order to practise this, you will need to play in a big open space and practise kicking the ball up high or in a specific direction. The kick can be taken from the ground where the ball is placed on its narrow end on a pile of sand or kicking tee. Alternatively, it can be kicked from the hands which is done to start the game or when taking a quick penalty.

A very large part of rugby is about finding spaces and avoiding being flattened by your opponents! You could practise running and changing direction quickly in many different ways. Here are a few ideas:

- Walk around an open space outdoors (or school hall if indoors) and when you hear a clap or whistle blow, quickly turn and walk in a different direction. Repeat several times but be unpredictable with your signals.

- As above but jog rather than walk, then progress to running.

- Rather than just turning on the signal, drop and touch the floor and push off in another direction at a run.

- Place obstacles like garden chairs or upturned flower pots around the open space and try to run around them quickly without bumping into them. Use a stop watch to give a greater sense of urgency.

- Carry a rugby ball with you as you run, run around three obstacles then pass the ball to a catcher.

- Play tag games.

- Play a shadow game. Play in pairs and try to lose your partner by making different moves forward, backward and side to side.

The physical contact in rugby is not introduced until secondary school so this should not be a problem if your child is still at primary school. They will be playing tag rugby where a ribbon or band is tucked into their shorts and the opponents have to catch the player and collect the 'tail'. This is quite a fun game to play anyway, with and without a ball. For young people having to play more physical games at school, you might consider joining a martial arts club, where the physical contact is much more controlled and you learn how to balance and stay on your feet or fall safely when tackled. Judo would be particularly good for this. It would also help improve posture, strength, timing, physical fitness and self-confidence.

If all else fails, don't forget to consider the role of the coach or official for your child. This will enable them to keep up to speed with the social chat and be part of a group.

R ## Resources

Barrington Sports: www.barringtonsports.com (UK)
    Telephone: +44 (0) 1565 650269
    Gilbert Skill Skin rugby ball leash and Gilbert XT500 training rugby ball

Early Learning Centre: www.elc.co.uk
    Football Target Game.

References

Johnson, P. (1997) *Crowood Sporting Guides: Rugby Union Technique, Tactics, Training*. Ramsbury: Crowood Press.

8 SKIP TO MY LOU

When we were growing up, as girls, it was definitely a 'rite of passage' to be able to skip. We would use all sorts of materials to skip with. The skipping ropes could be made of actual rope, washing line (which stung like mad if you twanged your legs with it!), and dressing gown cord. If you were posh, you had a proper skipping rope with wooden handles with ball bearings that stopped the rope getting twisted as you skipped. We would skip morning, noon and night trying to learn new skills and tricks!

Although we regard skipping as a girl's playground game, it is thought that it was originally a man's activity, as far back as the ancient Egyptians. It was in the early 1940s and 1950s that children from inner cities used jumping rope as a form of play. In more recent times, games such as this have taken a back seat to television; however, it is now gaining in popularity. In particular the British Heart Foundation promotes skipping as an excellent activity for getting a healthy heart. They have been working in partnership with schools to encourage skipping as part of PE lessons and during playtimes for all ages. The British Skipping Rope Association suggests that, as an organized activity, skipping can help with concentration and behaviour. This Association organizes an events calendar and skills workshops. See the Resources section for contact details, as there may be an event near you.

Skipping can be great fun and once you get going it is an excellent form of exercise. It can be a good social activity in that you can play it as a threesome with friends holding either end of the rope (this is called 'long rope'). If you use two long ropes at the same time, this is called 'double dutch'. It is also a game that you can play by yourself. You can skip to rhymes and do actions. You can learn rope tricks and skip to music. All you need is a good skipping rope. Ropes are inexpensive, portable and fairly easy to use. Jumping can happen virtually anywhere, inside or outside. Little space is needed for basic jumping skills. Children of all ages and skill levels find numerous ways to use the rope.

Skipping develops many skills:

- practises co-ordinating movement between upper and lower body
- instils a sense of rhythm and timing
- improves motor planning, as the mind and body have to work together to perform a complex sequence of movements
- improves balance
- develops speed and reaction times
- improves jumping, vertically and horizontally (upwards and forwards) for other sports
- increases flexibility
- exercises the back which also has quite a workout in this activity
- helps develop the arm muscles including the wrist and forearms
- improves stamina and fitness (body workout).

? Where does it go wrong?...those frustrating times

Some children find it hard to learn the basics of skipping and it is well worth just stepping back for a moment and seeing where it might be going wrong for them. Here are some things to consider before starting out:

- Can your child jump upward, forward, backward and sideways with both feet together?
- Is he able to jump on the balls of his feet in a bouncing rhythmical pattern?
- Can your child time his jump to coincide with the rope's position?

- Does your child appear to perceive the correct height of the rope and jump accordingly?

- Is your child able to initiate and maintain the twirling motion with the rope?

- Can he co-ordinate arms and feet together when turning the rope for himself?

Notes for grown-ups

When skipping, wear good 'jumping shoes', that is, no sandals or slippery shoes. Trainers are the best. Shoes should be securely tied before jumping.

Clothing should be comfortable but not baggy; hats and jewellery should be removed before jumping.

Tips and hints

How do we start? Here are a few ideas:

- Make sure the rope is the correct length for your child. Individual ropes are sized by holding the handles, one in each hand, and stepping on the rope. The handles should come up to the armpits. A 'skipper' may elect to use a shorter jump rope as he becomes more efficient.

- Beginner 'skippers' do better with 'beaded ropes', which tend to keep their shape well when turned. Because you also hear them 'hit' the floor it helps to establish a rhythm. Very lightweight cloth and plastic/vinyl ropes are harder to control because they do not keep a consistent loop.

- Getting the body position right is very important to jumping. Your child needs to stand upright with the head positioned squarely on the shoulders and eyes focusing straight ahead. The knees should be slightly bent and about shoulder width apart.

- A correct grip is essential when using the jump rope. The grip should be comfortable but firm. The elbows need to be close to the body and the wrists should remain slightly below the elbows when jumping in the rope.

- When turning your rope use small circular wrist movements (not large arm circles). Learning the rope swing is key, in order to keep the smooth and continuous flow of rope jumping.
- The use of music is a powerful motivator, whether used as background, or to help with the timing and rhythm needed.

Table 8.1 lists some of the things that can be problematic and possible solutions. Try some of the ideas that others have told us about that have helped their children.

Games to play

Before you start with skipping it is helpful to play some games which will develop your child's confidence in using the rope as well as the jumping skills needed. Here are a few ideas to help you with this.

Warm-ups
WHAT YOU NEED
Nothing

WHAT YOU DO

- Circle the arms as you would when skipping but start with small circles and gradually increase to full range of movement. Do this slowly and with control especially if your child has very mobile shoulder joints.
- Practise jumping with both feet together. This could be done on the floor or on a trampoline or indoor jogger.
- Practise hopping from one foot to the other on the spot.
- Hold the rope, folded in half, tightly between both hands, up above the head. Stretch the arms and body side to side in a slow movement.
- Sit on the floor with legs out straight in front, feet together. While holding the ends of the rope, place the middle of the rope around feet, between the balls and arch of both feet. Stretch the back of calves by pulling the rope toward you with your hands. Stretch the front of lower legs by pointing toes on both feet and allowing little resistance with hands holding the rope.

Table 8.1 Areas of difficulty in skipping skills

Difficulty	Possible reason/solution
Losing balance when jumping over the rope.	Ensure your child's starting position is correct – see above. This helps readiness to jump with the rope and has a good effect on posture for balance.
	Play some of the practice jump games above and below.
Jumping with both feet at the same time.	Remind your child to take off and land with both feet together.
	Practise bouncing on the balls of the feet.
	Practise some of the jump games above and below.
Coinciding the jump with the rope's position.	Practise the timing of skipping by jumping, landing, clapping, jumping, landing, clapping without the rope first.
	Practise some of the jump games above and below.
Judge the height of the rope as it comes towards the ground and jump accordingly.	Use a visual cue like fluorescent tape wrapped along the mid-section of the rope to help him see it more clearly.
Starting and maintaining the twirling motion with the rope.	Play music with a strong beat to help with the timing.
	Keep hands down beside and slightly out from the body.
	Use a hula-hoop instead of a rope to begin with.
	Practise walking or jogging whilst twirling shortened rope in each hand (see 'Round 'em up cowboy' game below).
Co-ordinating arms and feet together when turning the rope.	Use shortened ropes in each hand (long enough so that the looped ends touch the ground). Twirl the ropes using wrist action. As the rope hits the ground, encourage your child to jump.
	Cue him to bend his knees and jump each time he hears the rope hit the ground.
Is your child able to jump on the balls of his feet in a bouncing rhythmical pattern?	Use music with a strong beat to help with the timing.
	Practise jumping on a trampoline or indoor jogger to help get a sense of the feeling of continuous jumping.

Line jump
WHAT YOU NEED
Rope (use a chalk line if this is too difficult at first)

WHAT YOU DO
Stretch out the rope in a straight line on the ground. Starting at one end of the rope, jump side to side over the rope to the end. To make it harder try jumping backwards over the rope.

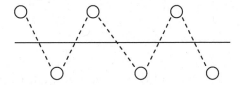

Jump high jump low
WHAT YOU NEED
Rope; two or three players (if you don't have a third player tie the rope to sturdy pieces of furniture, gate post or door knob)

WHAT YOU DO
The rope is held in a stationary position by two people standing one at each end (be sure that the rope is held loosely in the hands). Your child attempts to jump over the rope. Alter the rope's height after a few successes. Start with the rope on the ground. When it gets too high, try it limbo style!

Wiggly worm

WHAT YOU NEED

Rope; two or three players (if you don't have a third player tie the rope to sturdy pieces of furniture)

WHAT YOU DO

The rope is held at each end and wiggled to and fro making a 'wiggling snake' motion. The height and width of the moving snake can be altered depending on the ability of your child.

At the sea side

WHAT YOU NEED

Rope; two or three players (if you don't have a third player tie the rope to sturdy pieces of furniture)

WHAT YOU DO

The rope is held at each end and waves are made in the rope by moving the arms up and down. Your child attempts to jump over the rope at the lowest part of the wave.

Ring jump

WHAT YOU NEED

Rope with an object that can be tied to the end (an old sock with a tennis ball in is great); two players

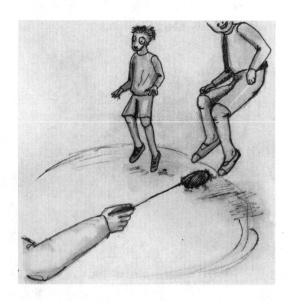

WHAT YOU DO

Hold the rope and then turn around so that your child has to jump over the rope as it passes by. Keep the rope close to the ground at first. To make it harder slightly increase the height. Start slowly and build up the speed. But don't get dizzy!

Round 'em up cowboy

WHAT YOU NEED

Rope

WHAT YOU DO

Shorten the rope by holding both ends together in one hand. Your child holds the rope at his side with the looped end touching the ground. The rope is twirled, using wrist action. As the rope hits the ground, jump. This helps to develop your child's ability to listen to the sound the rope makes when it hits the ground, which is a useful cue to prompt the 'jump'.

Try these other rope games to help your child get used to handling the rope in his hands and moving the rope around his body.

- *Helicopter* – hold rope above your head with both hands together. Make circular movements with your wrists, twirling the rope over your head like a helicopter. Kneel down and keep the rope spinning, then stand up again.

- *Windmill* – hold the handles of the rope close together and swing the rope in front of you in a circle (turn rope with your wrists not arms).

In and out

WHAT YOU NEED

Rope; two or three players (if you don't have a third player tie the rope to sturdy pieces of furniture)

WHAT YOU DO

Turn the rope in a consistent rhythmical manner. Encourage your child to run through the rope without letting the rope touch him (see the photograph below). To help cue him when to run, encourage him to listen to the rope touching the ground.

Skipping rope rhymes

Rhymes or chants work well to reinforce rhythm and timing. You will also see that skipping can also reinforce academic skills such as memory, spelling words and maths. Here are a few ideas for you to try, but check out the Resources section for some useful websites which have lots of other rhymes.

I love apples, red and green

Tasty fruit is fit for a queen.

Let us pick some from the tree

You can eat them along with me.

How many apples can we eat?

1, 2, 3, 4…

Salute to the Captain

Bow to the Queen

And turn your back

On the dirty submarine

1 and 1 are 2

2 and 2 are 4

4 and 4 are 8 (see if you can keep the skips going to do different times tables)

Mother, Mother, I am ill.

Call the doctor over the hill.

In came the doctor.

In came the nurse

In came the lady

With the alligator purse.

'Measles,' said the doctor.

'Mumps,' said the nurse.

'Nothing,' said the lady

With the alligator purse.

Chickety, chickety, chop.

How many times before I stop?

1...2...3...4...

My mother made a chocolate cake.

How many eggs did it take?

1...2...3...4...

ABCs and vegetable goop

What will I find in the alphabet soup?

A-B-C-D-E-F-G——

R Resources

42 explore: www.42explore.com

British Rope Skipping Association: www.brsa.org.uk

Fun and Games: www.funandgames.org

Kids Games: www.gameskidsplay.net

Streetplay: www.streetplay.com (US)

USA Jump Rope: www.usajrf.org (check out for useful links)

Woodlands Junior School: www.woodlands-junior.kent.sch.uk

Go to Amazon for a number of books on skipping or playground games.

References

Bissell, J., Fisher, J., Owens, C. and Polcyn, P. (1998) *Sensory Motor Handbook: A Guide for Implementing and Modifying Activities in the Classroom*, 2nd ed. San Antonio, CA: Therapy Skill Builders.

Skipping rhymes: www.saskschools.ca/~gregory/gym/skiprhymes

VanDyke, L. (2006) 'Jump Rope History'. www.buzzle.com/articles/jump-rope-history-health-fitness.html

Worknotes: www.worknotes.com/IL/Chicago/Fit4FunKidsFitness/ap16.stm

9 'FRENCH' SKIPPING... OOH LA LA!

When we were young girls (a very long time ago!) there was a great playground game which we played with our friends. We called it 'French skipping' but it may have other names depending on the part of the world you live in.

French skipping develops many skills:

- practises jumping
- helps with remembering sequences of instructions
- helps with rhythm and timing of movements
- co-ordination of the two sides of the body
- eye/foot co-ordination
- rhymes and counting
- turn taking
- develops an understanding of movement concepts (up, over, on, off, etc.)
- great for general physical fitness
- it is a social game because even if you are not so good at the jumping you can still join in and be an active part of the game by being one of the team who holds the elastic
- most of all it's fun!

What is French skipping and how do we play?

'French skipping' is played using a long piece of elastic and usually between at least three people. It can also be practised in the privacy of your own home if the elastic 'ring' is placed around the legs of two sturdy chairs!

The two ends of the elastic are knotted firmly together to form a long loop (you can buy these elastics commercially. They are sometimes called 'cat's cradles'). Two people step inside the loop and stand with it just above their ankles (the 'enders'). They stand opposite each other approximately 1.5 metres (5 feet) apart. They stretch the elastic into a rectangle shape by standing with their feet shoulder width apart (or wider if wanted). To start with, the elastic should be at ankle height. The jumper then has to perform different hops and jumps in, around and on to the elastic. These jumps can be done whilst chanting skipping songs and rhymes.

The jumps start off very simply and build up in difficulty. If there are other people playing, this activity becomes one to practise social skills through encouragement of the 'jumper' and turn taking.

As the 'jumper' becomes more proficient, the elastic can be raised further up the legs to challenge the skill level until they make a mistake or miss a jump and the next player takes a turn.

Notes for grown-ups
- Care should be taken when jumping so as not to trip.
- Do not use the elastic too high until you are able to jump accurately on to and over it well.
- Keep away from furniture that you could fall on to or over, etc.
- Make sure that the elastic is wide enough, or brightly coloured if vision is impaired, and tied securely to prevent it snapping open and hitting someone.

Playing the game

 ### *Tips and hints*

- If you cannot find a 'French' skipping rope in the shops, make one by either joining together a number of thick elastic bands or knot tightly a length of 'knicker' elastic.

- Make sure the 'elastic' is taught enough between the two 'enders'.
- If jumping over the 'elastic' is hard to do, practise first by drawing chalk lines on the pavement.
- Try stepping in/on/out etc in the sequence rather than jumping. To help reinforce the jumps when teaching the game, say the moves out loud whilst demonstrating.

Games to play

First of all you will need to develop your 'jump' library. Once these have been mastered they can be used to develop increasingly complex sequences.

The rules of the game are:

- if the child lands on the elastic when he is not supposed to, then he is out
- if he is trying to land on it and misses, he is also out
- after a miss, the jumper trades positions with an 'ender'.

The game keeps going until everyone is either exhausted or bored! These are some words to describe the 'jumps':

- 'In' – jump with both feet together inside the elastic.

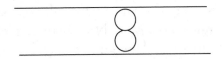

- 'On' – jump with both feet on top of the elastic. The left foot lands on the left elastic; the right foot lands on the right elastic.

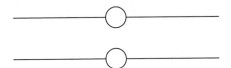

- *'Out'* (or *outside*) – jump with both feet together from the middle to the outside of the elastic. Feet land together on one side.

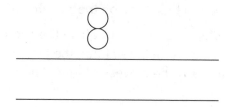

- *'Straddle out'* – jump and straddle! The left foot lands outside the left side of the elastic. The right foot lands outside the right side of the elastic.

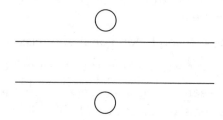

- *'Side jump'* – start with the left foot outside the elastic and the right one inside. Now jump so that the left is now inside the elastic and the right is outside.

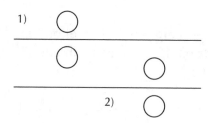

Jumpers call the steps out loud while jumping. Calling helps the jumper remember the 'sequence' of the jumps!

Make it harder...

- You now have the ingredients for hours of fun. Take turns to carry out each sequence. Use the 'doing' words as you describe what and where you are jumping. Raise the elastic to make you jump higher.
- Add several tasks together to make up your own sequences and give them a name.
- Have fun and introduce the activity to your friends once you have mastered the game for yourself.

Chants and rhymes

Rhymes or chants work well to reinforce rhythm and timing. Sequencing also helps to reinforce organizational skills. Academic skills such as memory, spelling words and maths can be developed at the same time. Now practise these simple jumping games with some of the ideas below.

England, Ireland, Scotland, Wales

WHAT YOU NEED
Elastic; three players

WHAT YOU DO
Start position – stand with both feet outside the elastic.

England – jump inside

Ireland – jump out

Scotland – jump in again

Wales – jump with both feet on the elastic

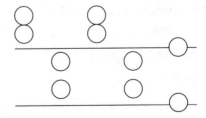

Chocolate cake
WHAT YOU NEED
Elastic; three players

WHAT YOU DO
Start position – left foot inside the elastic loop and right foot just outside. Here is one of the rhymes we say:

Chocolate cake, when you bake,
How many minutes will you take?
One, two, three, four.

On one: jump up and land with left foot outside the elastic and your right foot inside.

On two: jump up and land with both feet together inside the elastic.

On three: jump up and land with both feet outside the elastic.

On four: jump up and land with both feet on the elastic.

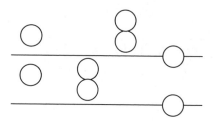

Mississippi
WHAT YOU NEED
Elastics; three players

WHAT YOU DO
Start position – both feet outside the elastic. The name of the game is to spell out Mississippi:

M – you jump into the centre

I – you straddle the elastic

S – jump to straddle left side of the elastic (side jump)

S – straddle right side of the elastic (side jump)

I – straddle outside the elastic again

SS – repeat the ss's as before

I – straddle outside the elastic again

PP – you step on the elastic both sides then double jump on it

I – jump outside the elastic again.

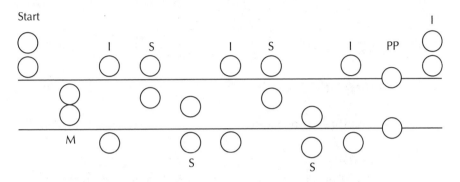

Ice cream soda pa-va-lo-va

WHAT YOU NEED

Elastic; three players

WHAT YOU DO

Start position – outside the elastic on the left side.

    Make the following jumps to match the syllables in this rhyme:

Ice – jump to straddle left side of the elastic (side jump)

Cream – jump with both feet into the middle of the elastic

So – straddle right side of the elastic (side jump)

Da – jump out of the elastic onto the right side

Pa – jump to straddle right side of the elastic (side jump)

Va – jump with both feet into the middle of the elastic

Lo – straddle left side of the elastic (side jump)

Va – jump out of the elastic

Start   VA

◯   ICE   LO   ◯

◯   ◯   CREAM   VA   ◯   ◯

    ◯   ◯   ◯   ◯

       ◯   ◯   ◯   ◯

          ◯   ◯   ◯

          SO   ◯   PA

            DA

Jingle jangle

WHAT YOU NEED

Elastic; three players

WHAT YOU DO

Start position – both feet outside of the elastic on the left side.
On each word make the following jumps:

Jingle – jump to straddle left side of the elastic (side jump)

Jangle – jump to straddle right side of the elastic (side jump)

Centre – jump with both feet into the middle of the elastic

Spangle – straddle outside the elastic

Jingle – jump to straddle left side of the elastic (side jump)

Jangle – jump to straddle right side of the elastic (side jump)

Out – Jump out

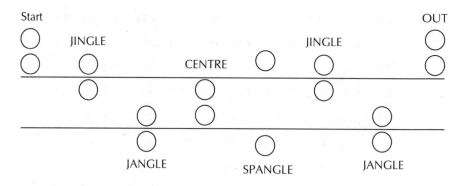

2, 4, 6, 8

WHAT YOU NEED

Elastic; three players

WHAT YOU DO

Start position – both feet outside of the elastic, on the left side.
  On each word make the following jumps:

2 – jump to straddle left side of the elastic (side jump)

4 – jump to straddle right side of the elastic (side jump)

6 – repeat 2

8 – repeat 4

Inside – jump with both feet into the middle of the elastic

Outside – straddle outside the elastic

Shut the gate – jump so that one foot is on each of the elastic

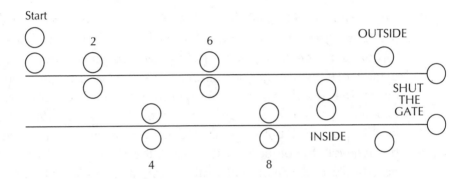

If you want more ideas, ask your mum, aunt, granny or another adult what they used to do when they played French skipping all those years ago!

Resources

Fun and Games: www.funandgames.org

Playground fun: www.playgroundfun.org.uk

References

Becky's Campfire Songbook: www.dragon.sleepdeprived.ca/songbook/
  songbook_index.htm (© Laurie and Winifred Bauer 2002)

Jump Rope Rhymes: www.everything2.com/index.pl?node_id=153452

NZ Playground Language: www.vuw.ac.nz/lals/research/playground/docs
  lip69.pdf (© Laurie and Winifred Bauer 2002)

10 GET YOUR SKATES ON

When we started to think about this chapter, we remembered the old fashioned grey roller skates which you had to wear strapped over the top of your shoes! They each had four wheels, ankle strap and you could make them longer or shorter by adjusting a screw plate underneath! They would only move quite slowly and didn't really allow you to experiment much. There were some other skates which had toe and heel brake blocks but generally we just had to run into the nearest garden wall, fall or learn to stop using the skates alone! Both of us have really fond memories of skating as children. We even tried 'Roller Disco' which was amazing fun but just as many bumps and bruises!

Needless to say, roller skating is another great activity which helps improve many of the areas of movement skills which your child may have difficulties with.

Roller skating develops many skills:

- balance
- co-ordination
- rhythm
- strength and flexibility in the legs and body
- improves posture
- gaining skills in this area also helps with other balance activities such as riding a bike or skateboarding
- physical fitness for hearts and lungs
- improves self-esteem

- it can be done alone or with a group of friends for fun where social skills and problem solving skills can be practised

- this activity is another one of those which once mastered can be developed into speed skating, artistic skating, inline or roller hockey and even ice skating.

Notes for grown-ups

As with other activities, there are safety considerations which need to be thought about before lacing up your skates:

Check the skates before skating: Make sure that brake stoppers are not loose or worn out, if you have them, wheels are free of dirt, grime or oil and are not loose, and that axles and nuts are tightened.

Skate on smooth ground: Check the surface and remove any sticks or stones. Watch out for potholes or cracks, broken paving slabs, wet leaves, water and loose gravel on roads and trails.

Stretch before you begin: Warm up thigh muscles, calves, hamstrings, hips and lower back. Your local children's physiotherapist should be able to help with advice or ask your PE teacher or a gym instructor at the local leisure centre.

 How do we get started?…before your child gets going on their skates

This is another 'fair weather sport' which can make learning a difficult new skill in the cold and wet make you want to give up!

 Tips and hints

- Consider which skates to buy first of all. Don't just buy the snazziest skates. There are three main types of skates:

  ○ *Inline hockey skates* are strong, allow easy turning and offer good ankle support.

  ○ *Speed skates* have a long wheel base and different wheels for different surfaces.

  ○ *Artistic quad skates* have two pairs of wheels sat one behind the other. They also have a toe stop (brake).

You might think that the four-wheeled, wide based skates would be best for starters but, according to the British Roller Skating Federation (BRSF), the toe stop can give a false sense of security or in fact lead to trips and falls.

- In addition to wearing protective pads and helmet it's a good idea to consider clothing too. It would be tempting to put your child in long trousers to protect his knees from all the tumbles but, unless they fit tightly around the ankles and lower legs, they can get caught in the skates and cause a fall. Bicycle clips do a good job when the trouser legs are wrapped around the leg first and clips then applied over the top. Horse riding suppliers sell lower leg 'half chaps' (known as 'gaiters' in Australia and America) which are elasticated, slightly padded, fluorescent leg protectors made to wear over slim trousers. *Tights* worn under trousers are another good option to protect the legs from the weather but also minor grazes. They keep the muscles warm. *Tops* should have long sleeves to protect elbows from cuts and grazes and offer warmth to muscles.

- Use a '*multi-sensory*' approach to teaching roller skating. This means giving verbal instructions – *say it*, visual demonstration – *show it*, and one-to-one hands on – *do it* instruction.

- Ask your child questions about what he is doing and how he thinks he can change his performance. We tend to retain information better if we have had to think about what it is we have learned and why we have learned it. However, try not to overload your child with too much information at one time.

- Always have fun. This should never become a chore.

Teach the basics

This is a very difficult skill to master, with plenty of spills and tumbles to graze the pride and knees, so your child will need to have lots of short practices. 'Little and often' is our motto. Try to learn one skill at a time so that you build up a repertoire of movements but at each new session go over what your child learned last time.

Before heading off to your local park or the front drive, it may help your child to 'feel his feet' with his skates on in the house first. Here are some more ideas to try first.

Tips and hints

- It is important to teach your child the basic positions and skills before he actually starts skating.
- He could start off by learning to walk and move around with skates on whilst indoors and on carpet.
- Your child can also practise the skating movements on a slippery surface such as linoleum or laminate flooring wearing socks and no skates. A good game is strapping paper plates to your feet and trying to 'skate' in them!
- Once your child has his skates on a less resistant surface, he may benefit from using 'ski poles', made out of two broom handles with rubber walking stick ferrules on the bottoms, to help with his balance.

The basic position

Begin with the skates on and stand up straight, placing the feet shoulder width apart with toes pointing slightly outwards (in a 'V' shape).

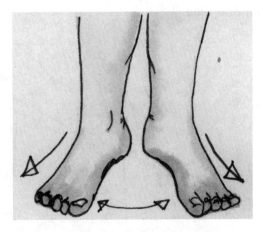

Next, encourage your child to bend his knees until he cannot see his toes any more (as though he is almost sitting on a chair). This next skill can be practised indoors with or without a chair for support. Being on carpet can give great resistance (more sticking power) and stop the skates rolling away with your child.

He should practise moving the body weight from one foot to the other whilst keeping both feet in contact with the floor. (You could try doing this to music to make it more fun and help develop the sense of rhythm needed later.) Next, he should try shifting the weight sideways but taking the non-weight-bearing leg slightly off the ground. Once he has understood this he is then ready to practise gliding from this position. Imagine pushing the moving foot along the side of a triangle from the narrow end up to the wide base. The opposite leg will also move along the 'side of the triangle' from the tip to the base, away from the body. Practise the movements yourself and 'feel' how your body moves and adjusts. This will help when trying to explain it to your child.

The flamingo

The second skill to teach is how to glide on one foot.

First, have your child try standing on their 'best foot' so that they can push off with the other leg. (Find this out before you start, by asking your child to stand on one leg and see which is their strongest.)

Encourage your child to push out with the free foot (the one your child is not standing on) and as the foot glides out, transfer the weight on to it. This will allow your child to lift the back foot and bring it up behind them like a flamingo. He should practise these movements on one foot at a time.

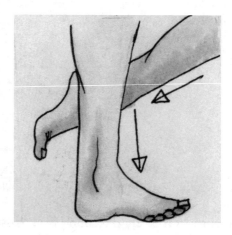

As confidence builds encourage your child to build up a rhythmic sequence, moving from side to side. It is at this point that you may want to consider using a 'handling belt' (see Resources) so as not to grab clothing or have your child grab on to you, which may cause you both to fall.

The T stop

Once your child learns to get going, he also needs to be able to stop. When learning to stop, he should practise the shape the skates form in order to slow down and stop. This is a letter 'T'.

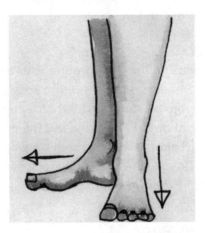

The front foot must face forwards and the back foot is brought behind the weight-bearing front foot at a 90 degree angle (pointing out to the side to make the top of the letter 'T'). There is more pressure on the inner border of the skate.

Once your child has mastered the correct foot position, he can try stopping from a basic glide. As confidence grows, he should try using the back foot in the 'T' position with gradual pressure on the inner border of the skate, then progress to slowing down gradually before coming to a full stop.

Games to play
Hokey Cokey
WHAT YOU NEED
Nothing

WHAT YOU DO
This is a nice activity to challenge balance and confidence in a more controlled game. Begin by singing to the tune of 'The Hokey Cokey', 'put your right hand in, your right hand out', etc. (see www.wikipedia.org for references and lyrics). Then push your right foot in, your right foot out...' and let him shake his foot all about; end the verse with a little jump.

Koosh balls
WHAT YOU NEED
Items such as juggling balls, koosh balls, rolled up socks, plastic fruit or shower scrunchies

WHAT YOU DO
Place the items on the floor around where your child is standing with his skates on. They need to be within easy reach for him to bend down to the front, to the side or just behind. Encourage your child to bend down to collect all the items and put them in a basket/box. For added fun they could aim them at a target. Begin playing this game on carpet and then gradually move to more 'slippery' surfaces. This game will help with balance and being able to adjust his body.

Going to the zoo
WHAT YOU NEED
Nothing

WHAT YOU DO
To encourage your child to move within the space he is working in, take advantage of his imagination and go on 'trips' as he manoeuvres around the space. It may be Disneyland or the circus. You may need to pantomime a bit as well to keep him motivated, as well as keeping a sense of humour in what can be a tense time for your child.

Stickers
WHAT YOU NEED
Some stickers

WHAT YOU DO
Place stickers on the floor for the child to skate towards. You can also stick them on his left/right hand to help with working out which side of the body he needs to move when learning the basics.

Moon rocks and boulders
WHAT YOU NEED
Nothing

WHAT YOU DO
Tell your child a story about how there is a giant rock in his way and there is no way around it. To get to where he needs to go (name a place) he needs to push this rock out of the way. As he 'pushes' it (arms out in front and head up) around the area, it continues to block his path. This game will help him to push strongly with his legs.

Red rover
WHAT YOU NEED
Nothing

WHAT YOU DO
Stand at one end of the space with your child at the other. Call to your child 'Red rover, red rover [your child's name] please skate over'. As he skates towards you stand with your arms out to the side (higher to start with) so that your child can duck underneath.

Red light green light
WHAT YOU NEED
Nothing

WHAT YOU DO
Your child stands in a starting position (triangle). On the command 'green light' your child begins to skate. On the command 'amber' your child gets ready to stop. On the command 'red light', your child stops. As your child gets confident mix up the commands and give them at a faster pace.

Mickey Mouse and co
WHAT YOU NEED
Some pictures of various characters or numbers or colours

WHAT YOU DO
Position the pictures around the space. Encourage your child to skate to a 'picture of...'. As your child gets more confident increase the distance apart, add obstacles or give the instructions more quickly.

Cargo

WHAT YOU NEED
A small object for your child to balance on his hand

WHAT YOU DO
The object of the game is for your child to get from point A to point B without dropping his cargo. This helps to keep the child's hands out in front of their body and his body erect.

Cones

WHAT YOU NEED
Small objects such as soccer training cones

WHAT YOU DO
Arrange the cones for your child to skate around. Start with a few, leaving large gaps between them. As he becomes more confident, add some more and decrease the distance. Add a time component to make it harder. See if he can beat his score each time.

Cliff hanger

WHAT YOU NEED
Chalk line

WHAT YOU DO
Draw a chalk line on the surface and explain that this is the edge of a cliff. Encourage your child to skate towards the 'cliff', but he must stop in time so that he doesn't go over it. Add other cliffs as confidence with stopping skills grows.

We hope this gives you some ideas to start with to help your child gain confidence on his skates. Check out the local leisure centres for any skating activities as well as the skating organizations listed in the information section.

R Resources

Skates and skating accessories

Allproducts: www.allproducts.com

Argos: www.argos.co.uk

Ashe Equestrian, the Equestrian Store: www.theequestrianstore.com (UK)
Neoprene half chaps.

Benefitsnow: www.benefitsnowshop.co.uk
    Comfy kids handling belt.
Skate Asylum: www.skateasylum.co.uk
Skate Warehouse: www.skatewarehouse.co.uk
Skater HQ: www.manlyblades.com.au
Skates.com: www.skates.com
Toys R Us: www.toysrus.co.uk

Information and coaching

British Artistic Roller Skating: www.rollerskating.org.uk
British Roller Sports Federation: www.brsf.co.uk
Roller Skating Resources: www.netaxs.com/people/grr/Roller/index.html (US)
Skate Australia: www.skateaustralia.org.au/rollersports
Skatelog.com: www.skatelog.com (various regions)

References

Simeone-Fondran, K. (2006) *Tips for Teaching Kids to Skate*. Accessed on 20/08/07 at www.iisa.org/icp/kids.html

Wilkie, K. (1999) 'Creative Teaching Methods for Instructing Children.' *Fitness and Speed Skating Times* (January). Accessed on 20/08/07 at www.fasst.com/articles/jan1999/jan1999-instructing.htm

11 BOUNCE BACK: REBOUNDING FOR FUN AND FITNESS

Trampolines are really popular and amazing fun for children and, more especially, adults! They are great for getting your heart and lungs working hard, for making your body stronger and more flexible. Let's face it, we all need to bounce to burn off the calories from crisps, sweets and fizzy pop that we know we shouldn't be eating and slurping.

In this chapter we are going to look at using a trampoline at home and an approach called rebounding.

？ What is rebounding?

Rebounding is gentle bouncing and guided movements on a trampoline, mini trampoline or even your grandma's bed! It is very different to gymnastic trampolining where somersaults and other stunts are performed. 'Rebound therapy' is the therapeutic use of the trampoline under the supervision of a physiotherapist or occupational therapist to work on a specific programme of activities to help improve particular movement difficulties.

Rebounding develops many skills:

- balance and co-ordination
- body and spatial awareness
- relaxation
- fitness levels and exercise tolerance
- language skills (through listening and use of words to describe the movements, and it also helps tone up the

muscles around the mouth and jaw which makes it easier to articulate words, so speech is clearer. The effects of this can last up to a few hours after the rebound session)

- concentration, listening and social skills
- following sequences of instructions
- confidence and self-esteem
- engaging in exercise which is fun and really motivating.

Learning to balance and jump on a trampoline may not be easy. Ensure that you are able to help your child and provide a safe environment for him to practise. This means that you should be confident moving on it yourself if your trampoline is big enough for two.

Notes for grown-ups
- Don't forget that a trampoline is a potentially dangerous piece of equipment and should be used in a safe way to avoid injury.
- Children with joint hypermobility (lax joints that are very mobile and 'bendy') should not be allowed on the trampoline without taking advice from a children's physiotherapist or their doctor first as the trampoline makes movements less controlled. This can cause your child to land awkwardly and damage joints.
- Ensure that your child wears loose clothing. Long trousers and long sleeved T-shirts are best with socks to protect the feet and toes. Ideally, the socks should have non-slip bottoms. Any ties, belts, scarves and jewellery must be removed to prevent cuts and tears, strangulation or damage to the items.
- Do not trampoline directly after a meal. Your child should not have sweets or chewing gum in his mouth. He should have a drink when he has finished (preferably not fizzy pop!).
- Only have one person on the trampoline at a time, as bouncing out of time with each other can cause the body to be propelled out of control into the air or off the trampoline. The only exception to this is when an adult is accompanying their child on the trampoline to help produce controlled movement.
- Avoid flip-flops and somersaults unless you are properly trained.

- Climb off the trampoline carefully to avoid nasty injuries from landing awkwardly or on someone else or an object close by.
- Place cushioning material all around and under the trampoline, such as bark chips.
- Keep the trampoline away from fences, trees, greenhouses and other garden furniture or play equipment.
- Use the safety nets designed for your trampoline, which should help prevent falls.
- Securely fasten a frame pad to cover the entire spring system, hooks and frame.
- Only use the trampoline when it is dry.
- Children should always be supervised by an adult. Children under six should not use large trampolines.

It is important to remember that although a trampoline seems like a 'toy', it is in fact a piece of gymnastic equipment and should be used in the same way as you would if you were using one at a gym club. This means *warming up slowly on the trampoline and stretching all your muscles beforehand.* You should also *'cool down' afterwards* (ask your friendly sports teacher or physiotherapist for some good stretching exercises to do).

Don't let your child 'overdo it' when on the trampoline. This is very easy to do because it feels as though you're not working very hard and it's so much fun!

If he experiences any unusual pain or discomfort that lasts for a few hours after trampolining, go and see your doctor who can refer you to hospital or a paediatric (children's) physiotherapist.

Getting on the trampoline and having fun
Tips and hints

- If using a large free standing trampoline, encourage independent mounting and dismounting, via steps or, once half on the trampoline, on his tummy, rolling on to the trampoline bed (rather like getting out of a swimming pool without using the steps). He should get off in a similar way by rolling to the edge with feet first and lower himself gently until his feet touch the ground. This activity alone is great for upper body strength!

- Encourage *movement* on the trampoline. For example: rolling, crawling, moving in 'high kneeling' (keeping the bottom up away from the heels), walking and slow running if size allows.

- Learn where the *middle of the trampoline* is. This is usually marked with a cross or circle for safety and orientation. If this is not there, mark one.

- *Gentle jumping* in the middle of the trampoline with feet together (if this is difficult it may be helpful for the adult to give some energy to the trampoline by pressing down with hands on the trampoline bed).

- *Increase duration* of gentle jumping (again if your child tires or finds this difficult the adult can give energy to help the child maintain the momentum and reduce failure, and push down on the trampoline to coincide with the jump).

- *Stopping*: after ten consecutive jumps encourage your child to make a controlled stop. This at first may require some practice; widening his legs (not too wide), keeping the feet in contact with the bed and making his knees relax (slightly bent) to 'soak up the "spring" from the bed' will help.

When your child has developed basic moving, jumping and stopping skills on the trampoline and is happy with his progress, play some of the following games.

Games to play

These games help the more confident 'bouncer'. If your child still finds the trampoline a bit scary then check out the games where the child is lower down on the surface of the trampoline, such as 'Rhino wrestling' or 'Frog on a lily pad'. Of course some of the other games can be adapted to play whilst just sitting on the trampoline until confidence is gained.

'Simon says'
WHAT YOU NEED
Nothing

WHAT YOU DO

This game helps improve body awareness whilst the child has to control their balance and maintain rhythm at the same time as bouncing. It's also a 'listening and doing', multi-tasking activity.

Whilst your child is bouncing, instructions are given such as: 'Simon says, put your hands on your head', etc. Build up the difficulty by adding instructions such as 'Simon says, bounce three times and put your hands on your head'. This helps with following instructions and with body awareness.

Catch and throw

WHAT YOU NEED

A medium to large-sized ball

WHAT YOU DO

Whilst your child is bouncing, encourage him to throw a largish ball with both hands. Begin to make it harder by decreasing the size of the ball. Depending on your child's age, try catching with just one hand, for example, just the right hand and then just the left. This is also good for eye/hand co-ordination and the throwing and catching skills needed in games lessons at school.

Twist and turn

WHAT YOU NEED

Nothing

WHAT YOU DO

Whilst your child is bouncing, give short instructions to turn, for example 'a quarter turn, then half turn to the left and the right'. Depending on the age of your child and their knowledge of 'left and right', you could start by pointing towards the direction you want them to turn. Add to this by using other directional concepts like north, south, east and west, and numbers which relate to each position (1, 2, 3, 4). You could always use landmarks to help with orientation, such as the tree, greenhouse, shed or house. This also helps with following instructions and directional concepts/ language, which is something the children will need in geography and maths in school.

Baton ball
WHAT YOU NEED
Sturdy cardboard tube; soft large ball

WHAT YOU DO
The child holds the 'baton' with one hand on either end. Throw a soft, biggish ball and get him to hit it back by using the 'baton' whilst bouncing on the trampoline. This also helps eye/hand co-ordination and helps with 'batting skills' in games lessons at school.

Opposites
WHAT YOU NEED
Nothing

WHAT YOU DO
Whilst bouncing, instruct your child to lift one knee up and touch it with the opposite hand, for example, left hand to right knee. Now try right foot and left hand, but this time he has to reach behind him. Don't forget to keep him bouncing! This will help with concepts of 'right' and 'left', following instructions and crossing over the body midline, which is important for body co-ordination skills.

Chase
WHAT YOU NEED
Nothing

WHAT YOU DO
If the trampoline bed is large enough, play chase on all fours around the trampoline bed. This helps with speed of reactions as well as movement control.

Pass around the world
WHAT YOU NEED
A small ball or an old pair of socks rolled up into a ball

WHAT YOU DO
Whilst bouncing on the trampoline get your child to take the small ball or rolled-up sock from one hand to the other around the body. To make it harder, he should pass it over one shoulder then the other, that is, your child will need to reach his other hand up behind the

back to collect it. He can also try passing it under one leg. Build up the sequences and the speed. This helps with co-ordination skills as well as body awareness.

Frog on a lily pad
WHAT YOU NEED
Nothing

WHAT YOU DO
This game can be done with your child on their own, on a small trampoline, but is much better on a much larger trampoline. Your child should be sat cross-legged whilst you walk around the trampoline bed trying to disrupt his balance! If he is too good, you could try bouncing a little higher yourself, which will make him topple over. The aim is to stay sitting with legs crossed and hands on the knees. Moving the hands or toppling over means he has to be the 'walker' and you become the frog! You can adapt the game by choosing a new starting position, such as kneeling on hands and knees or in high kneeling or long sitting (legs out straight in front). This not only helps with balance skills but also helps to work the muscles in the tummy and the back. It also helps to promote 'saving reactions'.

Trampoline twister

WHAT YOU NEED

Find or make a large cube and add the numbers 1–6 or colours on each face (this is your die)

WHAT YOU DO

Throw the die. Your child has to carry out the tasks relating to the number, for example:

1 = put one body part on the bed (e.g. stand on one leg)

2 = two body parts (e.g. stand on two legs)

3 = three body parts (e.g. stand on two feet and one hand)

4 = four body parts (e.g. stand on two hands and two feet)

5 and 6... Well, you can decide what to do next!

This will help with body awareness, balance, body organization and number skills.

Rhino wrestling

WHAT YOU NEED

Nothing

WHAT YOU DO

You will need to be on the trampoline with your child or use another child of similar size to play this game. You can start it in several different positions. For example, kneeling on all fours, the wrestlers should be side by side (head to tail). On the word 'go', each child or opponent should try and push the other over with their body weight. You can make it more difficult by walking around the wrestlers as a referee would do! This will challenge the children's balance even more. Another, but more difficult, starting position is in high kneeling facing each other, hands touching palm to palm (not clasping or holding) at shoulder height, elbows bent. The children use their arm strength to try to knock one another over. Also try this game sitting back to back.

Now see if there are some games that you and your child can make up. Have the best fun ever bouncing (why do you think Tigger was always so happy and fit?) but do it safely.

R Resources

There are many commercial retailers for trampolines, so check out the internet and local suppliers. The following sites may be helpful and some also offer other ideas for garden games.

Big Game Hunters: www.gardengames.co.uk

Springfree: www.springfreetrampoline.com.au

The Kids' Window: www.thekidswindow.co.uk

Trampolines: www.trampoline-resources.com (UK)

Check out your local sports centres or ask your local council for someone who has training in rebounding or trampolining for children with different needs.

References

The Chartered Society of Physiotherapy: www.csp.org.uk

12 'B' IS FOR BALANCE AND BALL

The exercise ball is a piece of equipment often used in sports and fitness training. It can also be used by therapists for rehabilitation. You may hear them called by different names such as 'physio ball', 'gym ball', 'Swiss ball' or 'therapy ball'. They are readily available and can be bought from local sports shops or even larger supermarkets and department stores.

Using an exercise ball can develop many skills:

- increase back strength, flexibility, and strength in the tummy
- improve balance and posture
- strengthen arms and legs
- stretching to help with flexibility
- relaxation
- co-ordination.

❓ What size ball should I get?

Before you try out the ball be sure to choose the right size and firmness. The more inflated the ball is, the more difficult the exercise move will be. Therefore, beginners should probably choose a ball that is softer, that is, not overly inflated. It is also important to choose the right size based on the height of your child. The ball manufacturer or your fitness centre can provide height guidelines. When sitting on the ball, the knees should be at a 90 degree angle, so that the pelvis is level with the knees. This will ensure proper alignment and balance for all of the activities that can be done with the ball.

Here is some general ball-to-height guidance:

Age/height	Ball size
Children 1–2 years	30 cm/12 inches
Children 3–5 years	35 cm/12 inches
5 years to 4 feet 8 inches (1.4 m)	45 cm/18 inches
4 feet 4 inches–5 feet 3 inches (1.3–1.6 m)	53 cm/21 inches
4 feet 11 inches–6 feet (1.5–1.8 m)	65 cm/30 inches

Notes for grown-ups

- Before trying these activities, check with your doctor or therapist to make sure that it is OK for your child to do them.
- If any activities cause your child pain – stop! Don't push too hard or attempt too much. Slow and gentle will get you there, so be patient.
- Keep the ball in a safe place and away from pets.
- Do not allow your child to use the exercise ball unsupervised.
- Do not use the exercise ball after eating a meal or whilst chewing sweets, etc.
- Make sure that there is enough space to use the exercise ball without risk of injury.
- Use the ball safely – keep a hand and an eye on the ball when attempting to sit on it.
- These balls will roll away very readily if you do not keep them under control.
- Use the pump supplied with the ball to inflate it.
- Wear trainers when using the exercise ball as feet can become slippery on carpet and laminated floors and you need them to be 'non-slip' in order to provide support.
- It is very easy for children to become overexcited when using the ball, so there is a higher risk of injury to them and possibly to you as you attempt to support them.
- Be mindful of your own posture and the amount of support you are giving your child when they are on the ball. It is easy to overstretch and twist, which can lead to back injury. Always keep close to the ball and your child, protect your knees by kneeling on a cushion and maintain an upright posture. Don't be tempted to stand whilst supporting your child as bending over and supporting an 'unpredictable' load will also put you at serious risk of back or neck injury.

Tips and hints

- The best working position is where you and your child face each other.
- Wear comfortable, non-restrictive clothes.
- Warm up the muscle groups before you begin the activities and have a stretch when finished.
- To help maintain balance when working, focus the eyes on a fixed point.
- If your child starts to lose balance, stop and let him reposition.
- Encourage your child not to hold his breath during tasks – encourage him to breathe 'normally'.
- Avoid using your ball outdoors. This increases the risk of puncture.

Games to play

When doing activities while sitting on the ball, you need to encourage your child to sit properly. We have called this 'sit up tall'.

Sit up tall...mind you don't fall

WHAT YOU NEED
Exercise ball

WHAT YOU DO
Sit facing your child. Make sure he is positioned with feet firmly on the floor and feeling comfortable and safe. When ready encourage your child to pose and make a funny face (use arms and body to help make it funny). Then say 'Sit up tall'. Now your child has to get his body back into the correct sitting position. Play again. Use this game throughout your play with the exercise ball to remind your child of the good sitting posture.

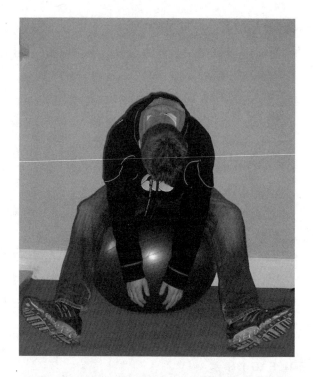

Sit up tall…mind you don't fall

Simon says
WHAT YOU NEED
Exercise ball

WHAT YOU DO
Whilst your child is sitting on the ball, play 'Simon says', which requires your child to move different body parts. Try to keep the ball still and feet rooted to the floor for support.

Catch and throw
WHAT YOU NEED
Exercise ball; ball to catch and throw

WHAT YOU DO
Play a simple throw and catch game whilst your child is sitting on the ball. You can also play aiming games, for example, throw a rolled-up ball of socks into a box or basket. You could also play a skittles game.

Bouncing ball
WHAT YOU NEED
Exercise ball

WHAT YOU DO
Sit on the ball with the feet firmly placed on the floor. Now start bouncing gently up and down on the ball. Next try to bounce whilst the arms are outstretched at shoulder height, then hold them up high in the air. This will make the activity more difficult. You can also put some dance music on and bounce in time to the music.

Cossack dancing
WHAT YOU NEED
Exercise ball; music

WHAT YOU DO
Use the starting position as described previously. Position the arms folded at chest height. Now extend each leg in turn to straighten, then bend whilst keeping the bottom and the ball still. When you have practised this, put on some music and dance like a Cossack (see the picture below).

Sitting hurdles
WHAT YOU NEED
Exercise ball

WHAT YOU DO
Use the starting position as described previously. Now extend out the right leg and stretch both arms above the head, then lower slowly to try and touch the toes on the leg that has been straightened. Repeat with the opposite leg. Try and keep both the ball and the bottom still.

Feed the dragon

WHAT YOU NEED

Exercise ball; box or basket to throw items into; rolled-up balls of socks or bean bags

WHAT YOU DO

The starting position for this activity requires your child to kneel behind the ball then slowly roll over the top of the ball until his hands touch the floor in front. The closer the arms are to the ball and the more of the body is on top of the ball the easier the activity is. If this is too easy, encourage your child to walk forward on his hands until only the thighs and the knees are only on the ball. Encourage your child to stay pushed up on the hands and not collapse on to the forearms. Now get him to move back to a point where his stomach is again over the ball. In this activity you can play bean bag target shooting games to 'feed the dragon'.

Push ball

WHAT YOU NEED

Exercise ball; two players; rolled-up newspaper or sturdy cardboard tube per player (baton)

WHAT YOU DO

Kneel on the floor with the bottom up off the heels and tucked in! Face a partner. Hold the rolled-up paper or tube with both hands (one at each end). Trap the exercise ball with the baton then hit it back to your partner with both hands on the stick.

Bridges

WHAT YOU NEED
Exercise ball; small ball, for example, tennis ball

WHAT YOU DO
Your child lies on his back with the feet up on top of the exercise ball. The ball needs to be supporting underneath the ankles. His arms should be kept down by the sides. See if your child can lift his bottom and thighs up to make a bridge. Roll a small ball under the 'bridge', then get your child to lower his bottom down to the floor slowly, with control.

Ball circles

WHAT YOU NEED
Exercise ball

WHAT YOU DO
Sit on the ball and place the hands on the ball for balance or place them on the knees. Slowly begin to roll the hips in a circle towards the right, then round to the left. Make small circles to begin with, and as this becomes easier try larger circles.

The puppet

WHAT YOU NEED
Exercise ball

WHAT YOU DO
Start by sitting on the ball with feet on the floor and the body and hands relaxed forwards like a folded puppet. Imagine that the main string to the 'puppeteer' is fixed to the top of the head. 'Feel' the puppeteer lift the head up until you are sitting up straight and tall. Next imagine that you have strings attached to the top of your hands, elbows, knees and feet. Imagine that the puppeteer has pulled your elbows then hands upwards. The adult can be the puppeteer calling out which parts of the body are being moved and where.

Seated march

WHAT YOU NEED
Exercise ball

WHAT YOU DO
Sit up tall on the ball. Begin a slow march, alternating lifting the right foot and then the left. As your child gets more confident, we can lift the knees higher and march faster. You can also add a bounce on the ball if he feels comfortable. Add some 'marching' music like the 'March of the Elephants' from the Jungle Book.

References

Beginner Exercise Ball Workout for Balance, Stability and Strength: www.exercise.about.com/library/blbeginnerball.htm
Swiss Ball Rehabilitation Concepts: www.logan.edu/faculty/rpvstl/swiss.html

13 LET'S GET PHYSICAL

Besides all the very specific activities we've given you in the book, we thought you might like some of the games that the children enjoy playing.

You could play one or two in isolation or you could link a few of them together to make a mini play session. The key is not to overtire your child with 'exercises', as they can seem boring and meaningless. This can reduce motivation and make the movement experience more 'therapy' than being fun and physical. Have a go yourself and feel which part of the body you are exercising! You could get the whole family involved with some of these games or invite a few of your child's friends around to play.

Games to play

Traffic lights
WHAT YOU NEED
Space

WHAT YOU DO
You need a small group of children for this. If you call out 'red', the children have to sit down. If you say 'green' they can run/walk, and if you say 'orange' they have to stand still. The leader calls out the colours in any order. The last person to follow the instruction is 'out'.

DVD
WHAT YOU NEED
Space

LET'S GET PHYSICAL / 145

WHAT YOU DO
This is a good game if there are a few children or adults playing. Find a space and change your movements according to instructions relating to the functions of the DVD. See if you can make up some others of your own.

- fast forward – run forward
- rewind – walk backwards
- play – walk forwards
- eject – jump up
- pause – stop

Push-ups
WHAT YOU NEED
Clear wall space

WHAT YOU DO
Stand in front of a wall or closed door at extended arms' length. Feet should be evenly spaced about shoulder width apart. Keeping body straight, lower top half until nose touches the wall.

Lower to count of five, hold for five an inch off the wall. Push back to five. Start with five repetitions and build up.

Also try half push-ups where your child is in a crawling position, hands directly underneath the shoulders. Lower the face to the floor then push the arms straight to lift the head up again to the start position.

Commando
WHAT YOU NEED
Room space; carpeted area; some obstacles to move under, for example, chair, coffee table or around cushions and under a duvet

WHAT YOU DO
Begin the game by getting on to the floor on the tummy. Encourage your child to crawl along the floor using his arms and legs to help him move. A variety of games can be played in this position, for example, races in teams, obstacle courses. Manoeuvre between, under, over low objects. The surfaces can also be of different textures. Be careful of knees and elbows when playing this game.

Push-ups

Half push-ups

Air chair
WHAT YOU NEED
Clear wall space

WHAT YOU DO
Stand against the wall and then slide down as if to sit on thin air. See how long this position can be maintained. Build up seconds over a period of time. This exercise is very important if you are going on a skiing holiday!

Bean bag mover
WHAT YOU NEED
Some 'bean bags' – these can be socks rolled up into balls

WHAT YOU DO
Have your child assume the 'crab position' (push up on to straight arms, lifting bottom off the floor). Carry a bean bag from one point to another.

Wrestlers
WHAT YOU NEED
Carpeted space; two players

WHAT YOU DO

For this activity you will need to work in a pair. Get into a high kneeling position (kneel up tall) and face one another with about an arm's length between you. Grasping each other's hands, so that they are bent up in front of them, you have to try and push each other over whilst keeping in the high kneeling position.

Hot dog
WHAT YOU NEED
A duvet or blanket; two players

WHAT YOU DO

The child lies on his back on the duvet/blanket and pretends to be a hot dog sausage. The other player is the 'chef' and rubs in pretend ketchup or mustard on to the hot dog. The chef then rolls up the 'hot dog' in the bread (duvet). Count to three and the hot dog then has to unroll. Make sure the head is not covered by the duvet.

Crawling races
WHAT YOU NEED
Space; selection of small toys; bin/box; two or more players

WHAT YOU DO

With a parent, sibling or friend, crawl as fast as possible down a pre-set course. Take a toy or bean bag from a stack with you and place it in a bin/box at the end of the course. Return to the start line and shout 'Finish'. If crawling on carpet, make sure the knees are covered over to prevent carpet burns.

Ping pong blow
WHAT YOU NEED
One table tennis/ping pong ball or airflow golf practice ball

WHAT YOU DO

Get into a crawling position (like a dog) and place a ping pong ball in front of your child's body. Blow the ball to a target at the end. Try not to sit back on the heels but make sure your child straightens up the arms after each blow (watch out for blowing out too fast and causing hyperventilation). Stand up slowly at the end of the race to make sure your child is not dizzy.

Step it up
WHAT YOU NEED
Some things to step up on to and off; space

WHAT YOU DO
Set out an obstacle course, where your child has to step over/on/off a series of obstacles. See if you can make them different heights. Get him to practise jumping off (be careful of course!). When your child gets really good at that, encourage him to collect some objects along the way, or see how fast he can complete the course. He can also try carrying some objects over the course on a tray.

Snail walk
WHAT YOU NEED
Small, lightweight box or basket; large bean bag or heavy blanket

WHAT YOU DO
Have your child crawling on all fours and place a 'shell' on their back, for example, large bean bag, heavy blanket. Have the child move around a maze.

Statues
WHAT YOU NEED
Space; music

WHAT YOU DO
Your child moves around the space to music using different speeds or types of movement, for example, walk, gallop, skip. Also use different directions – forward, back, etc. When the music stops, he must 'freeze' into a statue.

Roly poly
WHAT YOU NEED
Space

WHAT YOU DO

Encourage your child to lie out lengthways. Keeping arms above the head (so that they are on the floor not in the air) your child now 'log rolls' down the 'runway' trying to keep his arms and legs straight.

Magic room

WHAT YOU NEED

Clear wall space

WHAT YOU DO

Get your child to push the walls of the room to 'make the room bigger'.

Angels in the snow

WHAT YOU NEED

Floor space

WHAT YOU DO

Your child should try this game with eyes open, then with eyes closed. It was originally designed to be played in the snow (hence its name) but can equally well be played on a sandy beach (not such a good name!). Moving the arms and legs against the weight and resistance of the snow or sand helps improve body awareness and therefore enables the child to identify where their limbs are in relation to their body. In the absence of sand and snow, a carpeted floor will do the same trick.

1. Have your child lie on the floor on his back with arms and legs straight. He should slide his arms out sideways along the floor, and then return them to their original position.

2. Then he should slide his legs apart and return them to their original position.

3. Next he can move an arm and leg on the same side of the body. Return them to their original position.

4. You move one limb and ask your child to move the opposite limb into the same shape or position. He must have his eyes shut tight and no peeking. Repeat with other limbs and add sequences of movements too.

R Resources

British Gymnastics Fundamental Movement Ideas for Early Years: www.earlyyearsfundamentals.co.uk

Kranowitz, C. (1998) *The Out of Sync Child has Fun*. New York: Perigree Publishers.

My First Complete Book of Games. (Sterling Press: www.sterlingpublishers.com)

Rattigan, M. (2006) *Kidz Fiz Biz – Physical Business for Kids*. Carmarthen: Crown Publishing.

Russell, J.P. (1988) *Graded Activities for Children with Motor Difficulties*. Cambridge: Cambridge University Press.

Sport England: www.everydaysport.com

Wise, D. (2003) *Great Book of Children's Games*. Maidenhead: McGraw Hill Publishers.

14 CHILL OUT

After all the exercise (and what we did not say was that this was keep fit for the whole family!) we thought it might be helpful to have a few pick and mix cool-down activities to use at the end of your play sessions. It is as important to cool down physically and mentally after activity as it is to warm up. Some of the stretching and breathing ideas may also be helpful to relieve tension at the end of a busy day.

Games to play

Wash the dishes
WHAT YOU NEED
Space; another child

WHAT YOU DO
This activity helps to stretch the shoulder muscles. Your child will need to work in a pair. Stand facing one another holding hands. Chant the following: 'Wash the dishes, dry the dishes, turn the dishes over,' at the same time swinging the arms side-to-side. On the word 'over', swing the arms up overhead and turn around in a full circle, returning to the original position. Repeat several times.

Stretches
WHAT YOU NEED
Space

WHAT YOU DO
Stand with feet hip distance apart, arms stretched out to the side. Instruct your child to 'Stretch as wide as you can'; 'Squeeze all of your

body'; 'Now be soft like jelly'; 'Be stiff like a big tree... Now the gentle wind blows the branches... Now a big wind blows the branches to the ground'.

More stretches

WHAT YOU NEED
Space

WHAT YOU DO
Have your child sit on the ground legs extended and grabbing his feet (or as far down the legs as possible) with each hand. Through all of the following instructions, his hands cannot let go of his feet (this is another creative way to make the children stretch a bit).

Can you make one leg longer than the other? Now the other leg?

How wide can you stretch your legs?

How small can you make yourself?

How big can you make yourself?

Can you get your feet higher than your head?

Can you get your feet behind your head?

Can you stand and walk without letting go of your toes?

Picture this

WHAT YOU NEED
Carpeted space; pillow and duvet; soft music

WHAT YOU DO
This is like the game 'sleeping lions'. It's a game for a 'quiet time' and begins to use 'guided imagery'. Put the duvet on the floor or even on the bed. Encourage your child to close his eyes and get comfy. Play some soft music but turned down low. You should lower your voice and slowly say the following:

We're going to take a cloud ride.

Hop on a white, fluffy cloud.

Here we go up in the blue sky.

Do you feel the wind in your face? [Allow them to tell you how it feels.]

It's lovely, quiet and peaceful up here.

Now the cloud is floating down and lands you safely on the ground.

Now sit up slowly, sit for a moment and then have a drink.

Try a simple story which involves going for a ride on a magic carpet, sailing over the roofs and mountains.

Jelly
WHAT YOU NEED
Space; soft music

WHAT YOU DO
Your child lies on his back with eyes closed; turn off the lights and play the soft music. Work through the following activities:

Wiggle your toes and scrunch them up, now they feel like jelly.

Wiggle your legs, lift them up, now they feel like jelly.

Wiggle your hands, scrunch up your fingers, now they feel like jelly.

Wiggle all your body, now be still.

Count to five slowly and everyone sits up quietly.

Statues and rag dolls
WHAT YOU NEED
Space

WHAT YOU DO
In a standing position, ask your child to show you what statues look like (if necessary, remind them statues are often made of metal or stone). Now ask him to show you what rag dolls look like (if you've got one to demonstrate with, all the better). Repeat, alternating between the two. Continue the process with your child kneeling, sitting and, finally, lying down. Always end with the rag dolls!

'I'm melting!'
WHAT YOU NEED
Space

WHAT YOU DO
'Melting' is a wonderful, fun relaxation activity. Talk about the melting of ice cream and ice cubes with your child and then ask him to pretend

to be one of these things. Challenge him to show you just how slowly he can melt!

Balloons (for older children)

WHAT YOU NEED
See below

WHAT YOU DO
Breath control plays an important role in relaxation. When we inhale slowly and then exhale twice as slowly, we decrease the supply of oxygen and increase the amount of carbon dioxide in the blood, thus slowing down the activity of the nerves and brain. To promote deep breathing, you can ask your child to expand (by inhaling) and contract (by exhaling) like balloons, alternately (and slowly) inflating and deflating. Ask him to 'inflate' through his nose, with the mouth closed, and to 'deflate' by blowing out through his mouth (initially demonstrating with an actual balloon can help make this image more vivid).

Breathing straws: By using a straw your child can see how breathing feels. Have your child hold the straw in his mouth, with his hand near the other end. When he breathes in through his nose and out through his mouth, he will feel his breath on his hand.

Beach ball breaths: Hold up a deflated beach ball and have your child help you blow it up. This will teach him to breathe in and out a number of times in a row.

Magic balloons: Have your child pretend he has a magic balloon. Encourage him to breathe in through his nose and out through his mouth until he thinks his balloon is filled up.

Bubbles: Use bubbles to teach your child to blow through the wand (see bubble recipes in Appendix 3).

Hand lotion: Give your child a dot of hand lotion and have him rub it in. After it's rubbed in, have him smell it by breathing in through his nose.

Windmills: Have your child blow on a 'beach' windmill and watch it move as he takes a deep breath.

Elevator breathing

WHAT YOU NEED
Space and somewhere comfy to lie

WHAT YOU DO

Begin by encouraging your child to observe the natural inhalation and exhalation of his breath without changing anything. Proceed with the following directions:

Your breath is an elevator (use the word 'lift' if preferred) taking a ride through your body.

Breathe in through your nose and start the elevator ride.

Breathe out and feel your breath go all the way to the basement, down to your toes.

Breathe in and take your elevator breath up to your belly.

Hold it. Now, breathe out all your air. [Pause]

This time, breathe in and take your elevator breath up to your chest.

Hold it. Now breathe out all your air. [Pause]

Now breathe in and take your elevator breath up to the top floor, up through your throat and into your face and forehead.

Feel your head fill with breath. Hold it.

Now breathe out and feel your elevator breath take all your troubles and worries down through your chest, your belly, your legs, and out through the elevator doors in your feet.

[Repeat]

Outdoor silence

WHAT YOU NEED

Outdoor space and somewhere to sit

WHAT YOU DO

This simple activity will develop listening, imagining, describing and drawing skills. Find a place where you and your child can sit down outdoors. Once seated, ask for five minutes of silence. Explain that the animals and birds won't resume their activities unless all is quiet. Once the time is up, encourage your child to tell you about something he has never heard before. You'll be surprised at the answers you get – sometimes the quiet itself is something many children have never encountered.

Dance

WHAT YOU NEED
Space and some music

WHAT YOU DO
Use dance and acting/charades to promote the difference between tense and relaxed, for example, be a giant, be a fairy, be a tall building that cannot be knocked down, be a tree swaying in the wind...etc.

R Resources

British Wheel of Yoga, 25 Jermyn Street, Sleaford, Lincolnshire NG34 7RU;
Telephone: +44 (0) 1529 306851; Fax: +44(0) 1529 303223;
Email: office@bwy.org.uk

Feel Good Friends: www.feelgoodfriends.com

Relax Kids: www.relaxkids.com (UK)

Simply Kids Yoga: www.simplykids.com.au

Yoga Bugs: www.yogabugs.com (UK)

FURTHER READING

Addy, L. (2003) *How to Understand and Support Children with Dsypraxia.* Cambridge: LDA.

Biggs, V. (2005) *Caged in Chaos: A Dyspraxic Guide to Breaking Free.* London: Jessica Kingsley Publishers.

Boon, M. (2000) *Helping Children with Dyspraxia.* London: Jessica Kingsley Publishers.

Brookes, G. (2005) *Dyspraxia.* London: Continuum.

Colley, M. (2005) *Living with Dyspraxia: A Guide for Adults Living with Developmental Dyspraxia.* London: Jessica Kingsley Publishers.

Drew, S. (2003) *Jack and the Disorganised Dragon.* Cardiff: Dyscovery Press. (A story for children.)

Drew, S. (2005) *Adults with Developmental Co-ordination Disorder.* Chichester: Wiley.

Drew, S. (2006) *Including Children with DCD/Dyspraxia in the Foundation Phase.* Leicestershire: Featherstone Education.

Eckersley, J. (2004) *Coping with Dyspraxia.* London: Sheldon Press.

Edwards, N. (2004) *My Friend has Dyspraxia.* London: Chrysalis Children's Books.

Hunt, P. (ed.) and Byrne, M. (illus.) (1998) *Praxis Makes Perfect II: Dyspraxia: an Essential Guide for Parents and Teachers.* Hitchin: Dyspraxia Foundation.

Jones, N. (ed.) (2005) *Developing School Provision for Children with Dyspraxia.* London: Paul Chapman Publishing.

Kirby, A. (2003) *The Adolescent with Developmental Co-ordination Disorder.* London: Jessica Kingsley Publishers.

Kirby, A. and Drew, S. (2002) *Guide to Dyspraxia and Developmental Co-ordination Disorders.* London: David Fulton Publishers.

Macintyre, C. (2000) *Dyspraxia in the Early Years: Identifying and Supporting Children with Movement Difficulties.* London: David Fulton Publishers.

Macintyre, C. (2001) *Dyspraxia 5–11.* London: David Fulton Publishers.

Portwood, M. and O'Neil, J. (1999) *Developmental Dyspraxia: Identification and Intervention: A Manual for Parents and Professionals.* London: David Fulton Publishers.

Poustie, J. (2001) *Identification Solutions for Dyspraxia/DCD*. Cambridge: Next Generation.

Questions Publishing (n.d.) *Supporting Children with Dyspraxia*. Birmingham: Questions Publishing.

Reed, J. (2005) *Things that Go Bump in the Day: A Story about a Boy with Coordination Difficulties* (available from www.therapybookshop.com)

Ripley, K. (2001) *Inclusion for Children with Dyspraxia/DCD*. London: David Fulton Publishers.

Ripley, K., Daines, B. and Barrett, J. (2000) *Dyspraxia – A Guide for Teachers and Parents*, rev. ed. London: David Fulton Publishers.

Sugden, D. and Chambers, M. (eds) (2005) *Children with Developmental Co-ordination Disorder*. Chichester: Wiley.

Terrel, C. and Passenger, T. (2006) *ADHD Autism, Dyslexia and Dyspraxia*. Poole: Family Doctor Publications.

Velleman, S. (2002) *Childhood Dyspraxia Resource Guide*. New York: Delmar.

APPENDIX 1

Useful organizations for leisure activities and hobbies
UK

ARCHERY

Grand National Archery Society: www.gnas.org
Telephone: +44 (0) 1952 677888; Email: Enquiries@GNAS.org

ATHLETICS

UK Athletics: Kids:Zone: www.ukazone.net

BADMINTON

A useful alternative to tennis.
Badminton England: www.badmintonengland.co.uk
Telephone: +44 (0) 1908 268400;
Email: enquiries@badmintonengland.co.uk

BIRD WATCHING

Royal Society for the Protection of Birds: www.rspb.org.uk
Telephone: +44 (0) 1767 680 551

CANOEING

British Canoe Union: www.bcu.org.uk
Telephone: +44 (0) 115 982 1100

CLIMBING

Try climbing on an indoor climbing wall. You may find one at your local leisure
centre or try the British Mountaineering Council: www.thebmc.co.uk
Telephone: +44 (0) 870 010 4878

FENCING

One-on-one sport that develops lightning reflexes and a very strong body.
British Fencing: www.britishfencing.com

GO KARTING

This could be an alternative for children who have difficulty riding a bike.
Check out your local directory to see if there is a local centre.

GOLF

Golf Foundation: www.golf-foundation.org

HORSE RIDING

Horse riding is a great way to develop balance and co-ordination. Try local riding stables, also Riding for the Disabled Association: www.riding-for-disabled.org.uk
Telephone: +44 (0) 845 658 1082

JUDO

This martial art develops strength, balance, co-ordination and especially body awareness.
British Judo: www.britishjudo.org.uk

MUSIC

Youth Music: www.youthmusic.org.uk

ORIENTEERING

British Orienteering: www.bristishorienteering.org.uk
Telephone: +44 (0) 1629 734042

ROLLER SKATING

This sport comes in may different guises: free skating, roller hockey and inline speed skating.
British Roller Sports Federation: www.brsf.co.uk

SAILING

RYA Sailability: www.rya.org.uk
Telephone: +44 (0) 2380 627400

SOCCER

Use this website to find out more about youth soccer: www.thefa.com

SWIMMING

If you want to know where to find a good teacher or what swimming award schemes are available, contact British Swimming: www.britishswimming.org
Telephone: +44 (0) 871 200 0928; Email: customerservices@swimming.org

TAE KWON DO

This is another fabulous martial art that will improve balance, co-ordination, strength and flexibility plus *listening* skills!
British Tae Kwon Do Council: www.britishtaekwondocouncil.org.

TREASURE HUNTS

The National Trust organizes hunts in its gardens: www.nationaltrust.org.uk

WALKING

Get out in the fresh air and walk.

Ramblers' Association: www.ramblers.org.uk

YOGA

A fantastic way to relax whilst improving posture, breathing and composure.

British Wheel of Yoga, 25 Jerym Street, Sleaford, Lincolnshire NG34 7RU;
Telephone: +44 (0) 1529 306851; Fax: +44 (0) 1529 303223;
Email: office@bwy.org.uk

US

ARCHERY

National Archery Association

One Olympic Plaza, Colorado Springs, Co 80909;
Telephone: +1 (719) 578 4576

ATHLETICS

American Running Association: www.americanrunning.org

Telephone: +1 (800) 776 2732; Email: run@americanrunning.org

BADMINTON

USA Badminton: www.usabadminton.org

One Olympic Plaza, Colorado Springs, CO 80909;
Telephone: +1 (719) 866 4808; Email: usab@usabadminton.org

BASEBALL

Little League: www.littleleague.org

CANOEING

American Canoe Association: www.americancanoe.org

7432 Alban Station Blvd, Suite B–232, Springfield, VA 22150;
Telephone: +1 (703) 451 0141: Email: aca@americancanoe.org

CHESS

North American Chess Association: www.nachess.org

2516 North Waukegan Road, Suite 342, Glenview, IL 60025;
Telephone: +1 (847) 919 0431; Email: info@nachess.org

United States Chess Federation: www.uschess.org

Telephone: +1 (800) 903 USCF (+1 (800) 903 8723);
Email: uscf@uschess.org

CLIMBING

Rockclimbing: www.rockclimbing.com

277 Mountain View Drive, Brentwood, CA 94513;
Email: support@rockclimbing.com

CYCLING
USA Cycling: www.usacycling.org
One Olympic Plaza, Colorado Springs, CO 80909;
Telephone: +1 (719) 866 4581; Email: membership@usacycling.org

FENCING
National Office United States Fencing Association: www.usfencing.org
One Olympic Plaza, Colorado Springs, CO 80909–5774;
Telephone: +1 (719) 866 4511; Email: info@USFencing.org

GO KARTING
World Karting Association: www.worldkarting.com
6051 Victory Lane, Concord, NC 28027

GOLF
Get Good at Golf: www.getgoodatgolf.com
Pepsi Little People's Golf Championships: www.littlepeoplesgolf.com
Suggestions on equipment, training aids and lots of tips for the junior golfer:
Junior Golfers: www.junior-golfers.com

HEART HEALTHY CHILDREN
American Heart Association: www.americanheart.org

HORSE RIDING
Approved Riding Schools: www.approvedridingschools.net
Email: contact@approvedridingschools.net

ROLLER SKATING
Roller Skating Association International: www.rollerskating.org

SOCCER
American Youth Soccer Association National Support and Training Centre,
12501 S Isis Ave, Hawthorne, CA 90250; Telephone: +1 (800) 872 2976
US Soccer Federation, 1801 S Prairie Ave, Chicago, IL 60616; Telephone: +1
(312) 808 1300

SWIMMING
USA Swimming: www.usaswimming.org

TAE KWON DO
ATA National Headquarters, PO Box 193010, Little Rock, AR 72219;
Telephone: +1 (501) 568 2821

YOGA
American Yoga Association: www.americanyogaassociation.org

Australia

ARCHERY
Archery Australia: www.archery.org.au

ATHLETICS
Australian Little Athletics: www.littleathletics.com.au

BADMINTON
Badminton Australia: www.badminton.org.au

BASEBALL
(Little League) Baseball Queensland: www.qld.baseball.com.au

CANOEING
Australian Canoeing: www.canoe.org.au

CHESS
Australian Chess Federation: www.auschess.org.au

CLIMBING
Sport Climbing Australia: www.sportclimbingaustralia.org.au

CYCLING
Cycling Australia: www.cycling.org.au

FENCING
Australian Fencing Federation: www.ausfencing.org

GO KARTING
National Karting News: www.nkn.com.au

GOLF
Golf Australia: www.golfaustralia.org.au

HEART HEALTHY CHILDREN
Healthy Kids: www.healthykids.nsw.gov.au
Heart Foundation: www.heartfoundation.org.au

HORSE RIDING
Australian Horse Riding Centres: www.horseriding.org.au

ROLLER SKATING
Skate Australia: www.skateaustralia.org.au/rollersports

SOCCER
Football Federation Australia: www.footballaustralia.com.au

SWIMMING
Swimming Australia: www.swimming.org.au

TAE KWON DO
Tae Kwon Do NSW: www.tkdnsw.org.au
Tae Kwon Do Australia: www.taekwondoaustralia.org.au

YOGA
Find Yoga: www.findyoga.com.au

APPENDIX 2

How to make a pom pom ball
WHAT YOU NEED
Cardboard; wool

WHAT YOU DO
Cut two pieces of cardboard into circles then cut a circle out of the middle like a doughnut. Place the two pieces of card together and wrap wool round and round and round until the rings are full up. Snip the wool all the way around the outside edge, between the middle of the two pieces of card. Double up a separate piece of wool or string and looping it between the centre of the pieces of card pull it very tight around all the pieces of wool, effectively holding them all very tightly between the two bits of cardboard. Leave the tightening string long enough for you to use it to attach or hang the completed pom pom ball. Finally slide off the two bits of cardboard and ruffle the wool into a nice ball shape. Trim any stragglers with the scissors.

Use different pieces of coloured wool to form a multi-coloured ball.

APPENDIX 3

Bubble recipes

Here are some different bubble solutions for you to try. They all improve by being left for a day or so before using; we're not sure why, but they improve with age!

Basic bubble mixture

WHAT YOU NEED

- 20 fl oz water
- 1 fl oz washing-up liquid
- two dessertspoons glycerine
- Food colouring (optional, and for outside use only!)

All-purpose bubble solution

A good, all-purpose solution for most bubble tricks, experiments and activities.

WHAT YOU NEED

- 7 to 10 parts water to 1 part detergent (washing-up liquid)
- glycerine
- two teaspoons of caster sugar

Add ingredients and mix well.

Bouncy bubble solution

A fun solution that you can bounce off your clothes.

WHAT YOU NEED

- two packets unflavoured powdered gelatine
- 1 litre hot water (just boiled)
- 50 to 70 ml glycerine
- two teaspoons of caster sugar
- 50 ml washing-up liquid

Dissolve the gelatine in the hot water and then add the washing-up liquid and glycerine.

Note: You will need to reheat this mixture whenever you use it, as it will gel. Two to three minutes in a microwave should do it, but keep an eye on it the first time.

Thick bubble solution

A very thick, gooey solution that forms bubbles strong enough to withstand a small puff of air. You can blow bubbles inside of bubbles with this mixture and you don't need a straw. Just make a bubble and blow.

WHAT YOU NEED

- 2.5 to 3 parts water to 1 part washing-up liquid
- glycerine
- three teaspoons of caster sugar

Add ingredients and mix well.

A note about glycerine

Not all ingredients require the addition of glycerine in order to make good soap solutions. Glycerine helps soap bubbles hold water and this helps to keep the bubbles from popping. Try a tablespoon or so for a small batch (we're not exact about it). Glycerine can be purchased at most chemists. You won't need much, so don't go buying caseloads.

Bubble machine

WHAT YOU NEED

- a paper cup and drinking straw
- a piece of towelling material
- an elastic band or hair band
- bubble mixture

WHAT YOU DO

Make a smallish hole three quarters of the way down the side of the cup.

Put the end of the straw through the hole.

Stretch the material over the top of the cup and secure with the elastic band.

Make up some bubble mixture (as detailed below).

Dip the top of the cup into the bubble mixture.

Blow through the straw.

Hey presto!

INDEX